EPIC
BEGINS WITH
1 STEP
FORWARD

How To Plan, Achieve, and
Enjoy the Journey

Zander Sprague, LPCC

DEDICATION

*This book is dedicated to YOU, the reader! The fact that you
have decided to read this book is proof that you want an
EPIC life. I encourage you to pursue it, enjoy the journey,
and embrace your EPIC so you are open to receiving all the
wonder and enthusiasm the Universe holds in trust for you.*

CONTENTS

EPIC: *heroic, majestic, impressively great.*
Slang: awesome, spectacular, very impressive.

ACKNOWLEDGMENTS

I would like to gratefully acknowledge the following people:

My friends and family whose steadfast support has helped me in countless ways.

Aurora Winter for coming on this fantastic journey with me, for your support, guidance, and mentorship. Thank you beyond words for creating the Spoken Author™ method, recording podcasts together, and always believing in me.

Racquel Foran for your incredible gift of turning my musings, which at times rambled all over the place, into cogent prose that made this book come to life. Your writing and editorial skills are incomparable.

FOREWORD

Hi, I'm Aurora Winter and I've had the pleasure of knowing Zander Sprague for over a decade. I'm a serial entrepreneur, award-winning author, publisher, and trainer. When I host events, I dread the "zombie hour." That time when normally perky attendees become zombies in the afternoon: inattentive, and bored. But this never happened when Zander was speaking. His enthusiasm was so genuine and infectious, it would energize everyone—including me!

Zander is one of those rare people who makes everyone feel better. Not just reassured, but recharged. Not just recharged, but raring to go. Eager to tackle a bigger, bolder, more ambitious future than they'd ever dreamed of.

This impact is even more charming as Zander is innocent of the tidal wave of positivity he triggers by entering a room. He is genuine and uncontrived, sincerely seeking the best for everyone.

Seeing this magical quality, for years I encouraged Zander to bless the world with his gifts as a speaker. Sometimes it seemed he could not see what was so obvious to me—and to a room full of event attendees enchanted by his spell.

Finally, at an event I hosted in San Miguel de Allende, Mexico, in February 2020, Zander took a decisive step forward. He committed to writing a book for a mainstream audience that would launch his speaking career to the next level by providing a taste of what he is like as a motivational speaker. With my help as his mentor and book shepherd, he began writing.

And then the 2020 pandemic struck. Remember that? Conferences and events were canceled. International travel was canceled. Uncertainty skyrocketed and businesses slashed expenses. Could there be a worse time to launch a career as a public speaker?

Would the pandemic rob Zander of his dream? Would it rob the world of a great motivational speaker? While Zander loves to talk, he finds writing a chore. I worried that his new business and book would stall.

I love Zander like a brother, so I thought long and hard about his challenges and opportunities, his strengths and weaknesses. Entrepreneurs solve problems. How could I solve problems so that Zander could leverage his strengths and profit from his opportunities? How could I help Zander create his pivotal new book in a fun, fast, and joyful way?

That's when the concept of Spoken Author™ was born. I imagined creating a blueprint for the right kind of book, and then recording each chapter in a podcast episode. The podcast would then be transcribed, forming the basis of the first draft. While most people who write a book end up with only one book after years of effort, the best part of this new Spoken Author™ plan was that it would produce not only a book but also a podcast and an avalanche of social media content. The hours of audio and video content we recorded could be spliced and diced to create hundreds of pieces of short content for social media. This arsenal of content would then be leveraged to trigger prepublication media buzz and launch the new book.

Many books fail because all the effort is put into the book itself, and zero thought or effort is put into the book launch. I didn't want that to happen to Zander. The podcasts brainstorming his book would showcase Zander's energy and content, making it easy for him to get appearances as a speaker. The podcast would jump-start Zander getting scheduled on other podcasts, radio, and TV as a guest expert. This media coverage would enhance the growth of his business as an internationally acclaimed motivational speaker.

When I explained my Spoken Author™ plan to Zander, he loved it. Which was not surprising, as I designed it specifically for him. He was willing to be my first client through the Spoken Author™ process. Pandemic or no pandemic, Zander would not forfeit his EPIC goals!

Zander took a bold step forward and we started recording podcasts immediately. What I didn't realize at the time was that Zander was the catalyst for me to take a transformative step forward, too. I'm forever grateful that Zander was willing to boldly go where no one had gone before. Now I help many people write their books the Spoken Author™ way, thanks in no small part to Zander's enthusiasm. He helped pave the way for others to follow in his slipstream. Which is how Zander shows up—he makes the way easier for others—and a lot more fun.

Now you know the creation story of *EPIC Begins With 1 Step Forward: Plan, Achieve, and Enjoy the Journey.* The book you hold in your hands is like having Zander as your own personal coach. My nickname for Zander is the "God of Enthusiasm" so you have an outstanding champion on your own EPIC journey.

Aurora Winter, MBA
Best-selling author, *Turn Words Into Wealth*
Founder, www.SamePagePublishing.com

INTRODUCTION

I think we can all achieve amazing, extraordinary, and breathtaking things. EPIC things! But we are also vulnerable to getting stalled, discouraged, or losing faith in ourselves. We can be plagued by self-doubt and tripped up by the Imposter Syndrome. We can be derailed by unexpected losses—from global setbacks like the 2020 pandemic—to more personal tragedy. We can lose precious momentum wondering, "Who am I to have an EPIC life, business, and impact?"

If you have ever experienced any of these things, you are not alone. I have been there. More times than I can count! But I weathered the storms and achieved EPIC things by taking one step forward. And so can you.

My goal with this book is to be your personal coach and champion, cheering you on toward achieving your most cherished dreams, desires, and destiny. I suggest you read this book one chapter at a time, and then work on the EPIC Actions that accompany each chapter. The more you engage with this book, the more valuable it will become. Think of me as your coach—which means that you have got the ball. You are the player on the field. Your life is a participatory sport, so make sure you take part in it!

By reading this book and applying it to your life, career, and relationships, it will transform you. It will empower you to make EPIC choices—and build an EPIC life.

You will discover:

- How to discover, visualize, and realize your EPIC goals
- How two magic words will immunize you from feeling discouraged
- How to build upon your strengths
- Ways to acknowledge your awesomeness
- How to turn failure into feedback
- Ways to delegate and build your dream team
- How to plan, achieve, and enjoy your EPIC journey!

Reading this book is your first EPIC step. This book, along with the *EPIC Begins* podcast, and the *EPIC Begins* Now website (epicbeginsnow.com website) will be your blueprint to planning, achieving, enjoying, and celebrating your dreams. Let the EPIC adventure begin!

EPIC Choices, EPIC Life!

CHAPTER 1

EPIC CHOICES, EPIC LIFE!

THE WORD EPIC IS BIG. I have always liked it for that very reason; it is evocative of doing something enormous, exciting, and outside our comfort zone. EPIC challenges us to live up to our full potential. In reminding you that your EPIC journey all begins with just one step, hopefully the challenge will feel less intimidating and more doable. But by presenting the word in all caps—EPIC—you will not forget how big and exciting your dream is.

The word EPIC conjures monumental images, but that is because we use the word to describe events or experiences that impress us outside of ourselves. The skill of a professional athlete amazes us, and a surgeon saving lives awes us, but rarely do we stop and think about the EPIC things we do in our own lives. Mostly, because we do not see our achievements as EPIC. But many of them are. If you are doubting yourself, it will help to remember the EPIC things you have already achieved in your life. If you have accomplished one EPIC thing, then you can achieve more!

For me, it was an EPIC achievement when I ran my first marathon, and another EPIC achievement when I wrote my first book. Admittedly, these are impressive achievements, but I accomplished each by tackling them one simple, manageable step at a time. I simplified my BIG EPIC dream by creating a series of smaller milestones I could achieve along the way.

Choose Your Goal

It might surprise you how choosing our goal is often the biggest roadblock of all to pursuing our dreams. People dream big but play small. We have grand ideas and wild dreams, but then water them down to where they become washed out. It is important that you clearly know what your goal is so you can achieve it.

> *It is easier to determine where you are going if you have thought about exactly where you want to get to.*

For example, my goal is to be a motivational speaker before audiences of thousands. It is a clear, specific goal. Your goal might be to lose weight, tour East Asia in the summer, start your own business, or retire early. The point is to choose and clearly define your goal. Do not say I want to lose weight; say I am going to lose 20 pounds. Do not say I want to retire early; say I am going to retire by 60. Do not say I want to go to East Asia one day; say I will go to East Asia this summer. Do not say I want to be a public speaker; say I want to be a motivational speaker in front of audiences of thousands. It is easier to determine where you are going if you have thought about *exactly* where you want to get to.

Set a Deadline

It is important to impose a deadline on your goal. Someday is not a deadline and, therefore, you are unlikely to achieve your goal if you leave that open-ended timeline. Depending on your goal or dream, some deadlines might be easier to determine than others. If you want to lose 20 pounds, you could set a goal of losing 4 pounds a month for 5 months. So, your deadline for losing 20 pounds is 5 months from the day you take your first step. But if you want to start your own business, you probably need to factor in a lot of different things, so you would likely have to do some research to determine your deadline. Either way, setting a deadline is key to achieving your goal. If you do not set a target for achieving your goal, you are more likely to put it off indefinitely.

Sometimes the deadline for your goal will seem so far off in the distance it is difficult to envision. This can be discouraging. For this reason, also set a deadline date for each step of the journey. For example, one step to achieving my dream of growing my public speaking audience was to record the *EPIC Begins With 1 Step Forward* podcast, so I gave myself a deadline for when that project should start, and another for when I wanted it to be completed. Then I broke this down with further deadlines: a deadline for acquiring recording equipment and a deadline for editing each podcast after recording.

When you set specific goals with set deadlines, you are more inclined to achieve them. And remember, every

100% Commitment Makes You Happier

A 2002 study published in the *Journal of Personality and Social Psychology* found that although people prefer to make decisions that can be changed later, this may not actually make them feel happier.

Photography students were split into two groups: those who had to make an irrevocable choice about which print of theirs they would like to keep, and those who could choose but knew they could change their mind later.

(continued on next page)

step you take is meaningful on your EPIC journey.

Go for It!

Sometimes the fear of the unknown, or the fear of failure, prevents us from going for it. But if you spend some time thinking about it, you find that the times in your

(continued from previous page)

Despite believing that having flexibility in their choice would make them happier with their choice, this did not turn out to be the case. Those who had a choice liked their selected print less than those who did not have a choice.

life that you felt most inspired and exhilarated were when you fully committed and took the plunge.

When I was about 12 years old, we went to a quarry where we jumped off a 60-foot cliff into water. I stood on the edge and felt scared. It terrified me, but I stepped off the cliff anyway. In that moment, the thing that went through my mind was "I'm fully committed. I can't change my mind. Gravity has got hold of me. I can't grab onto anything. I can't stop this." So, I did fully commit to it because I did not have another choice. I made the best of the moment and clearly survived.

That decision on that day led to a lifelong journey of adrenaline-inducing adventures. I love doing stuff that scares me and pushes me. I have done bungee jumping and skydiving. I ride my road bike downhill as fast as I can because I love that feeling, the rush. If I had not taken that plunge when

I was 12, I might never have discovered this part of myself.

Commit and go for it! If you fail, that is okay. You are trying. None of us is ever 100 percent successful at everything we do. **The only thing you can be a hundred percent sure of is that you will fail at everything you do not try.**

Find Your People

Accountability to others drives us. When I wrote my first book, *Making Lemonade: Choosing a Positive Pathway After Losing Your Sibling,* which is about my experience with my sister's death, I sat on it for five years. I said, "Oh, I am coming out with a book." But I was no more coming out with a book than flying to the moon. The book was complete, but I was not really doing anything to publish it.

I do not see myself as a writer, so although the fact I wrote a book was amazing, I did not believe that people would like what I had written. But I felt accountable to others. I told people I had written a book. I did not want to be one of those people who, for 20 years, said he was coming out with a book but never does. Many of us get stuck like this, though. It is easy to talk the talk, but difficult to walk the talk. We have big ideas and plans that we shuffle around for months, years, even decades, but never act on them. We dream big but then do not know how to get where we want to be, so we just keeping dreaming and talking.

Things change when we tell people about our plans. Eventually it wore on me I had told so many people about my book it forced me to act. The same thing happened when I tackled my first marathon. Once I told friends and family that I was running a marathon, I felt I could not back out of it. Most of us like to do what we say. I had asked people to donate. I said I was running, so I was now accountable to those people. Finding people who hold you accountable but also support and believe in you is a big help in achieving your goal. Once you decide to go for it, you do not need or want to be surrounded by a bunch of naysayers. If you can find a mentor or coach, that is great, but at least find a friend or family member who will help keep you on track and encourage you and your efforts; even when things are not going as planned.

Do Not Be Stopped by Roadblocks

We all get slowed by roadblocks. We get stuck, often on stupid things. Before I tried to run a marathon, I was so hung up on the 26.2 miles that I was missing the fact that if running a marathon was easy, I would have already done it. Because something is difficult should not be a permanent roadblock. Nor should the potential for failure be a roadblock.

> *Trying will not guarantee success, but not trying will guarantee failure.*

Here I think about Olympic athletes. They train for years, decades even, to reach the podium. However, despite the time, effort, energy, blood, sweat, and tears they sacrifice, many never reach it. Fourth place, although notable, does not hold the prestige of a medal. Does this mean those athletes who did not win should not have bothered trying? I do not think so. Trying will not guarantee success, but not trying will guarantee failure.

My journey is a good example. A few years ago, I was facing a triple threat of challenges. My marriage, career, and education were not fulfilling. I was working as a speaker but was not having the success I wanted. I knew that I had to earn a master's degree to gain the credibility I needed to achieve my speaking goals. Because my marriage was not going well, I struggled to find motivation to make a change.

I was faced with a choice. Do nothing, settle for an unfulfilling life, and let my dreams remain unfulfilled. Or find the courage to change. I chose to change—one step at a time. The day I made that decision was the beginning of the rest of my life. After much therapy and soul-searching, with a heavy heart, I decided to get a divorce. I chose to proactively pursue the education I needed to become a Licensed Professional Clinical Counselor (LPCC). It turns out that starting was not as difficult as deciding to start. One step the first day, another the next, and another the day after that.

I completed my licensing internship hours at the end of February 2020. By the middle of March, we were in pandemic lockdown, and we could not leave our homes. This made pursuing my dreams more challenging. I found myself frustrated with my progress and unhappy with my apartment. I tried to take the LPCC exam, but the scheduling offices were closed. I tried to book speaking gigs, but companies were uncertain about the future, and venues were not scheduling events, so no one was hiring speakers. I was not living the EPIC life I envisioned when I took that first step several years earlier.

I sat alone in my apartment eating my way through the pandemic, when I had an epiphany: *EPIC Begins With 1 Step Forward!* I already understood that change begins with the first step. That is how I got where I was. But the epiphany was that I needed to make EPIC choices to have the EPIC life that I envisioned. EPIC choices create EPIC results. When I implemented this idea in my life, everything changed for me. And when you implement it in your life, everything will change for you too.

Fast-forward a year and my EPIC choices have brought me closer to the EPIC life I was dreaming of. I now live in a gorgeous home. I am dating a woman I love. I got my degree as a Licensed Professional Clinical Counselor, and I am working hard on my goal of becoming a renowned speaker. I am spending my time doing what energizes me. When I implemented EPIC choices in my own life, I got EPIC results.

I did not let roadblocks stop me. During a global pandemic, I decided to begin my EPIC journey to become a motivational speaker and inspire and uplift thousands of people. There were no crowds of thousands while I wrote this book. People could not gather, stadiums were shuttered, and events canceled. This appeared to make my goal impossible. I could have said, "Oh, I can't do this right now," but that would have been a cop out. Instead, I found a different way to achieve my EPIC dream. The pandemic was an unexpected detour, not a permanent roadblock.

I admit, I did not know how I was going to achieve my goal, but I knew I was on the EPIC journey, and I had taken some steps forward. The amazing thing is, it was not nearly as difficult as you might think to take those initial steps. You simply need a plan that you can execute. If I can do it, you can too!

" *You can only travel the road before you one step at a time.* "

When pursuing your dreams, you will meet with constant and shifting roadblocks. When we are uncertain or fearful about the road in front of us, the roadblocks stand out more than the detour. There is always a detour to be found, though. If you set clear goals and then tease apart each decision you must make, the road before you will become clearer. Focus your energy on accomplishing one task. You can only travel the road before you, one step at a time.

Take Bite-Size Pieces

" *When we eat a pizza, we do not eat it all at once.* "

Instead of being overwhelmed by the scope and size of your goal, or focusing your attention on the roadblocks, redirect your attention to one step you can take. I like to use the Pizza Analogy. I love pizza. But when I eat a pizza, I do not eat it all at once. I slice it up and eat exactly the portion I want, one piece at a time. That is how we eat any kind of food, in bite-size pieces in the quantity we want. Rarely do we shove everything into our mouth all at once.

Why? Because if we do this, we become bloated and overwhelmed. We miss the creative nuance of flavors and no longer enjoy what we are eating. As with food, when you break your goals down into bite-size pieces, it becomes a lot easier to tackle and more enjoyable too.

> *When we are open to creativity, we receive creative ideas.*

As soon as you stop worrying about achieving your entire EPIC dream and commit instead to taking just one step, the floodgates of creativity, ideas, and opportunity will open. When we open ourselves to creativity, we receive creative ideas. If open to receiving them, anyone can have a flash of insight or a lightning bolt idea at anytime. Break down your goal into bite-size pieces, do one thing, and see how momentum builds and inspiration follows.

Believe Positive Feedback

While on your journey, listen to and believe positive feedback. We are all guilty of believing negative reviews and criticisms while denying the validity of positive ones.

When I finally released my first book, people told me how much they liked it, how helpful it was. "REALLY?" I just did not believe it. Now, had they told me the book was not worth the paper I printed it on, I would have believed that instantly.

It took me too long to believe the positive feedback. Do not make the same mistake of falling into Imposter Syndrome where you do not believe in yourself and what you offer. If you think you are an imposter, then so will others. **Believe in yourself and the good things others are saying to and about you.**

Appreciate All Your Journey Offers

" *Step into your life as the hero of your own journey.* "

Imposter Syndrome

Imposter Syndrome is when a person does not believe they are as good at or capable of things as others think they are, despite proven success. It is a voice in their head that says they are going to "get caught" as being a fraud or failure.

People who suffer from IS share common traits including self-doubt, self-sabotage, attributing their achievements to luck or external events, and being overly critical of their own work and achievements.

While working to achieve your EPIC goal, view the journey as your friend. When facing an uncertain road to our destination, we often place all our focus on the destination and begrudge every step of the journey. But if we learn to embrace the journey, befriend it, we benefit much more from what it offers. Even perceived problems can present new opportunities.

Through the process presented in this book, I encourage you to step into your life as the hero of your own journey. Reframe success as the journey itself. Before taking your first step, you were doing nothing, going nowhere. By simply deciding to take one step, you have achieved something. That alone is success. Stop the negative self-talk, release victim energy, and soak in every phase of your journey.

" *We make things more difficult than they need to be. Take that first step!* "

Take my interest in running a marathon as an example. I had always wanted to complete a marathon but doing so seemed impossible. Thinking about running 26.2 miles was daunting, and I did not know how to get started. I kept focusing on that long 26.2 miles and that big number stalled me from training for even one mile. I was so focused on the goal being impossible that I never even considered the other achievements I could celebrate along the journey. I was making things more difficult than they needed to be. I knew I simply had to take the first step.

When I took one step toward my goal of completing a marathon, it set me on the path to achieving it. I did some research. I found Team in Training with The Leukemia Lymphoma Society, and I joined. Taking that first step led to two things: first was they gave me a training schedule to follow. That was a big deal, because now I had a schedule and bite-size pieces I could manage. My schedule said go for a run for 30 minutes on Tuesday, so I did. I did not think about the marathon or wonder how I was ever going to run 26.2 miles. I just thought about going out for that 30-minute training run.

The second thing that happened was team fund-raising. Doing this meant that I had to tell friends and family that I planned to run a marathon. This committed me. When we state our intentions to others, we feel more on the hook to deliver. Having a goal, along with accountability to people, made the training process easier. Once I embraced the training process and celebrated each achievement along the journey, the goal felt within reach.

What is your goal? Do you want to run a marathon, climb a mountain, save for an EPIC trip, or earn a degree? Whatever your goal is, define it, set a deadline, and think about one step you can take toward achieving it. When you do this, your EPIC journey will have begun!

"My roadblocks are a mirage. They don't exist; therefore, I am free to move forward."
ZANDER SPRAGUE

EPIC ACTIONS

1. Choose a goal.
   - Determine exactly what it is you want to achieve.
2. Set a deadline.
   - Set a date by which you want to achieve your goal.
3. Get an accountability partner.
   - Find a mentor, coach, trainer, or friend you can make yourself accountable to.
4. Visit www.EPICbeginsnow.com to learn more EPIC Actions you can take.

CHAPTER 2

FIRST EPIC STEPS

" *... you do not need to know the answer to every 'How do I...?'* "

A LL JOURNEYS BEGIN with the first step. First steps can feel like the most difficult, but remember EPIC is not necessarily huge or complicated. We become so overwhelmed with the thought of everything there is to do, we end up doing nothing at all. We get stuck on "How do I...?" But here is a not-so-secret secret: you do not need to know the answer to every "How do I...?" Doing something can be scary, so we default to failure before we even try to succeed. Instead, I want you to commit to one step. And we almost never take only one step, so trust me when I say one successful step will lead to the next one.

See Your Dream

Spend some time framing your goals and visualizing your dreams. You cannot arrive at your destination if you do not know what it is. You have stated your goal, now what does the end picture look like? In my case, the big end picture is one of me standing on a stage in front of an audience of 1,000-plus people who are truly engaged in what I am saying. Overlay photos in my mind include me being on a nationally syndicated television show talking about how to achieve EPIC goals. The dream is BIG and **bold** and might seem like a fantasy to some, but I am committed to it.

What does your **BIG,** bold dream look like?

British Army Adage

7Ps: Proper Planning and Preparation Prevents Piss Poor Performance

Develop Your Plan

    You need to know your destination, but also understand that there are many routes to getting there.

You must have a plan to achieve your EPIC goal. Consider the steps involved in executing your plan. You need to know your destination but also understand that there are many routes to getting there. Roadblocks, detours, and more than a few potholes will disrupt your journey. The more planning you can do, the better off you will be in the long run. As the British Army 7Ps say: "Proper Planning and Preparation Prevents Piss Poor Performance." Although you do not need to know (and it is probably impossible to know) every necessary step in advance, before you start, know your direction, and have a rough road map of steps to get there.

To achieve your plan, you must commit to it. Without committing all your energy, heart, and determination to your goal, it is difficult to achieve EPIC. Jack Canfield, author of *The Success Principles,* says, "A 99% commitment to something is very hard, 100% commitment is easy." And this is true. When you commit only partially, you leave wiggle room for yourself and opportunities for excuses not to do things to seep into your plans. You have no choice but to make the best of the circumstance when you fully commit, as I did when I jumped off the cliff.

> *No Exceptions Rule*
>
> "Successful people adhere to the 'no exceptions rule' when it comes to their daily disciplines. Once you make a 100-percent commitment to something, there are no exceptions. A 99% commitment to something is very hard, 100% commitment is easy."
>
> Jack Canfield, *The Success Principles.*

When you find your direction and have fully committed to your goal, ask yourself:

- What am I able to do?
- What is within my power and abilities to accomplish?

If you put your mind to it, you will realize there are a lot of things you can do to get started. For example, when I started thinking about becoming a professional speaker, long before I set my current goal of expanding my audience, I had absolutely no idea where or how to begin. So, I took one small step. I looked up professional speaking associations and discovered the National Speakers Association. And sure enough, they had all kinds of resources to help me get started.

When I decided I wanted to be a coach, I mentioned it to someone at an event where I was promoting my book about sibling loss, and that person suggested I reach out to Aurora Winter. I took that step and the next thing you know, I had signed up to be a grief coach.

In both my examples, before thinking about what I wanted to do and setting a clear goal, I had no inkling what steps to take. How could I? I had not thought about where I wanted to go. However, as soon **as I knew where I wanted to go, the steps to get there became clearer.**

Simplify the Steps

Often, we focus so much on how big our goal is we stumble before we start. When working on any task or goal, it is best to simplify the steps as much as possible. When I decided I wanted to run a marathon, I started with some basic research. This research led to me finding Team in Training. Joining the team led to a training schedule. Once committed to training, I started fundraising for the team. Fundraising led to making myself accountable to people who donated on my behalf. This accountability was a driving force behind continuing the training and breaking down my goal into simple steps: first a half marathon, then mile 17, then mile 20, then mile 26, until finally I only had to make it 0.2 more miles to achieve my goal. And that last 0.2 miles was a killer, but not nearly as brutal as staring down the initial 26.2 miles goal. I believe if I had continued to focus on that huge number alone, I probably never would have run a marathon, let alone four of them.

> *It is okay to be clear on what you want, but not on how to get there.*

I approached writing my first book, *Making Lemonade: Choosing a Positive Pathway After Losing*

Your Sibling, much the same way. Writing a complete book was an EPIC goal, not a step. Because I do not consider myself a writer, I had to figure out how best to accomplish my goal without becoming discouraged by the committee of naysayers in my head. If I was going to write the book, I knew I had to break down the process to something more manageable. In that case, dictation was the fix. Although I prefer speaking in front of a crowd, dictating my ideas into a microphone was better than writing them out! So, I paced around my office and dictated my thoughts and experiences about sibling loss until I had recorded enough to fill a book.

Committing to dictating one hour a day was a regular step I could take toward my larger goal. Once again, I am not sure I would have ever completed the book had I continued to focus all my thoughts on the fact that I am not a writer. Instead, I found something simpler I could do, broke it down into steps, and then began taking those steps one at a time until I reached my goal.

When I first embarked on those journeys, I was clear on what I wanted, but did not know how I was going to get there. And that was—*is*—okay! That did not prevent me from taking one step toward my goals. **Once I took the first step, the momentum grew.**

What steps can you take toward your goal? Are there organizations with resources you can access? Is there research you can do to help you get started?

Focus on the Task at Hand

> " *I have not met a person yet who can write a book with their right hand, while simultaneously doing math with their left.* "

Do not create an impossible scenario for yourself by taking on too much all at once. In our effort to do it all, we often accomplish nothing. I have not met a person yet who can write a book with their right hand, while simultaneously doing math with their left. Despite this, we think we must try to do this. If you try to multitask like this, though, you will do nothing particularly well, and you will end up feeling frustrated and overwhelmed.

A good way to approach your EPIC goal is like you would baking. You would not measure and mix the ingredients of a cake before ensuring you had them all. Can you imagine turning on the oven and then going to the store to buy flour? Then when you get home, you discover you needed eggs too. And then when you returned from buying the eggs, you discovered you needed sugar!

To successfully bake a cake, you need a recipe, you need to make sure you have all the ingredients and tools required before you begin, and you must follow the instructions and order of the recipe exactly. You cannot think about what you need to complete a task while you are working on the task. And you cannot complete the task if you do not have the tools and resources you need in hand. Planning and preparation allow for better use of your time and better execution.

When following the road map of your EPIC journey, like a recipe, you must chunk up your steps and then tackle them one at a time in the most logical and practical order. For example, I could not start recording the *EPIC Begins* podcast without a microphone and recording equipment. It would have made no sense for me to sit down to record my first podcast without having the equipment. It also would have made no sense to record the podcast if I did not know what I wanted to talk about. So, getting the equipment I needed and writing a podcast outline were obvious and relatively easy first steps I could take one at a time.

Remember also to stop when you have taken your step. It is usually counterproductive to do too much at once or push ourselves beyond our limits. When writing my first book, I could manage committing to one hour of dictation a day. However, if I consistently went over that hour and gave myself a sore throat from talking too much, then this might have led to me breaking my routine of daily dictation. It is better to stop when you have achieved what you set out to do, so you are fresh and ready to take another step the next day.

You will find blocking off dedicated time to accomplish specific tasks will increase your overall productivity and keep you on track to achieving your EPIC goal. For me, editing the *EPIC Begins* podcasts is a big job. When I first started my EPIC journey, I did not schedule dedicated time for editing and before I knew it, I was staring down half a dozen podcasts. The backlog made it easier to put off the task because when I looked at the entire project, I could never come up with a big enough block of time to complete it all. Instead, to get the job done, I needed to chunk it up and then schedule dedicated time to complete each chunk.

How can you schedule your time to ensure you tick things off your to-do list? Are there times of the day that are more productive for you than others? Develop a schedule that works for you and stick with it!

Ask for Help

When you visualize your goals, one thing you will quickly discover is that as many abilities as you have, there are those you do not. No matter how smart, talented, and hardworking you are, no one is a master of everything. As important as it is to make a list of things you can do, it is equally important to make a list of things you cannot. Then make a list of people who you can ask for help with those things.

One of the significant discoveries you will make with this step is that people genuinely like helping others. And if you present your idea with passion and enthusiasm, they usually cannot resist but get excited right along with you. It is crucial, though, that you are specific when seeking help. When reaching out to Aurora Winter for help with this book, had I simply said, "I need help," she would not have known what I needed or how to help. When asking others for help, it should not be incumbent on them to figure out what it is you want or need.

There is a great political story from Boston where I grew up. Tip O'Neill was a member of the House of Representatives for 34 years. The story goes he was at an event when a woman approached him and told him she did not vote for him. Tip asked why. She responded, "because you didn't ask." Through all his campaigning and speaking engagements, he apparently never simply asked for people's vote. The lesson here is that there is more harm in not asking than there is in asking, but also, be specific about what it is you are seeking.

For me, I needed help to get my speaking engagements to the next bigger level. I asked Aurora for help because I knew she had helped many entrepreneurs to get their million-dollar message out to the world and grow their businesses. Why would I not ask for help from someone who has experience helping others do exactly what I want to do? It was a bonus that Aurora had been encouraging me for years to take this step; we always want to add cheerleaders to our team.

When you ask someone for help, you are still doing the hard work, but you are inviting someone onto your team who can bring experience and insight into areas you might be lacking. If they have taken the journey before you, even if only partially, they can help you make your road map. You might know you want to drive from New York to Los Angeles, and you know you must head west, but there are many routes to your destination. Adding someone to your team who can help determine the pros and cons

Asking for Help Leads to More Success

Startup Genome is a policy advisory organization for public and private agencies whose goal is to speed up the success of the start-up ecosystem. The organization issued its first Startup Genome Report in 2011. Among the relevant findings was that tech start-ups that have mentors, track metrics, and learn from other start-up thought leaders raise seven-times more money and have three-and-a-half times better user growth than those that do not.

of each route can save you a lot of wasted time and energy.

For example, it is not a good idea to take the Interstate 90 in the dead of winter because you are likely to run into ice storms and blizzards. Also, not a good idea to drive the Interstate 10 in the middle of summer because it crosses through the Mojave Desert where the temperatures can surpass 100 degrees. Venturing out on your journey without this information in hand could lead to disaster. Not that you will not arrive at your destination if you take the wrong route in the wrong season, but it will be a far less treacherous journey if you have the best information in hand before you set out.

There are also many tasks you can delegate to others. Ask yourself before taking on a new task, is it the best investment of your time? Will spending your time this way help you achieve your goal by your deadline? Too often we try to travel our journey alone, but there are things we do not know or that others can do better and faster. If you ignore this, you will end up spending hours needlessly toiling away on problems. But when you simply put your problem out to your community, even through social media, it is amazing how quickly you can get answers and find help. In doing so, you save yourself hours and hours of spinning your wheels and can focus your energy instead on doing more productive things.

It is also important to remember when asking for help to ask the right people! Your success depends on you weeding out the killjoys. You do not need to surround yourself with a bunch of people who are constantly reminding you that, "You'll never do that!" Or saying you are insane and will end up, "Living in a van down by the river." When looking for team members, seek cheerleaders, not antagonists.

There is nothing easier to put off than the things we think we are bad at and the things we do not enjoy. So, **find your people, ask for help, delegate tasks, and focus your energy on what will get you to your goal the fastest and easiest way possible.**

Seek Joy in the Journey

When you embark on your EPIC journey, you must remind yourself that it will not be an easy one. I do not say this to be discouraging, but to prepare you for the road ahead. There are few things I can guarantee along the way, except that the unexpected will happen. It might be an amazing unexpected, challenging unexpected, or tragic unexpected event, but regardless of its form, unexpected things will happen, and it is during those times it is easy to fall off course. Remember to be kind to yourself through-out the journey. Forgive yourself your missteps. Do not let frustration overwhelm you when things do not go as expected. Shutdown negative self-talk and embrace the journey. Celebrate your achievements along the way and do not get too dragged down by the low moments.

All journeys have ups and downs, peaks and valleys, twists and turns, and light and dark. How many other journey analogies can I throw out here? The point is, embrace it all. You are on a journey, and it is exciting and there will be setbacks and unexpected occurrences, but that does not mean that you are not still on the journey to your destination.

> "   *Our entire life is a journey; shouldn't we be enjoying it?*   "

Anyone who has traveled internationally knows that missing one connecting flight can completely throw off your well-planned itinerary. And arriving in a new city is not a lot of fun if your luggage does not arrive at the same time as you. But instead of allowing these things to ruin your entire trip, you can view the unexpected as an opportunity to do something different from the usual. A delay in the airport might allow you to enjoy a fabulous meal at one of the terminal restaurants. Not having luggage gives you an opportunity to shop for things in stores you might not otherwise have visited. Neither of these things might have been part of your plan, but there is no reason these minor unexpected events must ruin or stop your journey. Our entire life is a journey; shouldn't we be enjoying it?

> *"If you really want to do something, you'll find*
> *a way. If you don't, you'll find an excuse."*
>
> JIM ROHN

EPIC ACTIONS

1. Make a list.
   - What is your EPIC goal or dream?
   - What does your dream include?
   - What does your dream look like?
2. Choose your first step.
   - It does not have to be complicated—the first step in taking a drive is getting in the car.
3. Once you choose your first step, plan it.
   - Preparation reduces the chance of failure.
4. Stop when you have achieved each step.
   - Doing one thing at a time is enough.
   - Enjoy each step of the journey.
5. Join the EPIC community at EPICbeginsnow.com.

CHAPTER 3

EPIC DREAMS DESERVE EPIC ANNOUNCEMENTS

YOU HAVE IDENTIFIED a goal you want to achieve, or a dream you want to bring to life. You have committed to it. You have laid out a plan or road map, and you have found your people. Now it is time to be brave and own it all! Announce to the world with conviction what you are going to do. Not what you are *hoping* to do. Not what you are *planning* to do. Not what you are *thinking* about doing. But what you are *going* to do. **Boldly proclaim your intentions and dreams!**

Believe Bigger is Better

When we are bold in stating our intentions, it shows enthusiasm, and others cannot help but feed

Goal Achievement Study

In 2015, Dominican University psychology professor Dr. Gail Matthews conducted a study entitled: *The Effectiveness of Four Coaching Techniques in Enhancing Goal Achievement: Writing Goals, Formulating Action Steps, Making a Commitment, and Accountability.* The study included 267 participants; 149 completed the study. They randomly split participants into one of five groups: Group 1- Unwritten Goal; Group 2- Written Goal; Group 3- Written Goal & Action Commitments; Group 4- Written Goal, Action Commitments to a Supportive Friend; or Group 5- Written Goal, Action Commitments & Progress Reports to a Supportive Friend.

(continued on next page)

off that enthusiasm. **Bold** is big, bright, and loud. There is fun in going BIG and being **bold**. The energy of boldness is the catalyst that will push you forward; the momentum of your **bold** goal will propel you further than you imagined.

When being bold, bigger is always better. Saying I am going to write a blog article about achieving EPIC goals would not be very bold. One blog article does not sound very EPIC. To say, however, that I am going to write a book about achieving EPIC goals and then embark on a mission to speak to hundreds of thousands of people about the topic does sound BIG and **bold**!

In some ways, bigger and bold is easier to achieve than small and safe. If my goal is to write one article, what then? And how difficult is that? Do I really need to pre-pare and research? Suddenly, the simplicity of the goal becomes the very excuse not to do it. So, do not water down your goals. Keep your eye on EPIC, whatever it is you are trying to achieve.

" *Have BIG, **bold** dreams, and ask BIG, **bold** questions, if you want BIG, **bold** results!* "

When you dream bigger, you think bigger and ask big-ger questions. If my goal is to sell 1,000 books, then my question is likely, how do a get 1,000 sales? If, however, my goal is to sell ten times that, 10,000 books, now my question must become more complex. What value does my book bring and who does it bring value to? If I can answer those questions, I am much more likely to hit my goal of 10,000 sales than to reach 1,000 with

(continued from previous page)

The results found that those who sent weekly progress reports to a supportive friend (Group 5) accomplished significantly more than those in the other four groups. At the end of the study, 43 percent of Group 1 were at least half-way or more to completing their goals. Sixty-two percent of Group 4 participants were half-way or had fully accomplished their goals. However, 76 percent of those in Group 5 either accomplished their goal or had at least half-way. Dr. Matthews concluded, "My study provides empirical evidence for the effectiveness of three coaching tools: accountability, commitment, and writing one's goals."

the basic question. Basic goals generate basic questions and ideas. If you want BIG, **bold** results, have BIG, **bold** dreams, and ask BIG, **bold** questions!

When you boldly proclaim you are going to do something, it puts you on the hook to do it. If you tell others you are going to do something but then never do it, you look a little foolish. We have all met big talkers. The people who are always telling stories about the next grand thing they are going to do, but each time you see them they are on to something new, never having achieved the previous thing. People like that lose credibility quickly, and we are all aware of this. Most of us want others to see us as credible people who do what we say we are going to. Stating to others with certainty and confidence that you are going to do something puts the pressure on you to deliver on what you are saying.

Own Your BIG Dream

A common roadblock to pursuing our EPIC goals and dreams is that we think our ideas are too big, unrealistic, or difficult to achieve. We focus on how BIG the goal is and on how we do not know how to start or how to achieve what we are dreaming about, so we chip away at that big dream, making it smaller to the point it does not even look like our original dream. Instead, make the steps to achieving your dream smaller and more manageable, not the dream itself. Keep the dream BIG! You have visualized what your end-result looks like, do not lose sight of that vision. Just because you do not know how to do something or how to get somewhere does not mean you should not try.

When I wrote my first book about my sister, Lucy and sibling loss, I did not know how to write a book. I certainly did not consider myself a writer, and before deciding to write the book, I never thought I would write one. The idea for the book came from having coffee with a friend of mine whose brother had recently passed. When I asked how she was doing, she made an offhand comment that there were a ton of books on loss of a spouse, loss of a parent, loss of a pet, but there were really no books on sibling loss. When I walked away from that conversation, I said to myself, "Hold on. I could write a book about that." So, I wrote the book, but then sat on it for five years because I was afraid to put it out there.

Writing this book was a different experience than my previous one. I was clearer about where I wanted to go and what I wanted to achieve. I boldly proclaimed that I was going to ramp up my speaking career, ramp up my book sales, and ramp up all of who I am to share it with the world. I reached out to Aurora, who has experience helping people create, share, and manifest their million-dollar message. That made me accountable. I took one step and things fell into place.

" *We all can do whatever it is we choose to do.* "

I had an incredible amount of time during the pandemic to think about what I want my life to look like. I realized I was tired of being small. And tired of making excuses for why I could not do something. I know and believe that we all can do whatever we choose to do. We simply must take that step forward and do it.

If you wait until your fear and uncertainty subside before pursuing your dreams, you will never pursue them. Do not let fear of the unknown stop you. Acknowledge your fear, but do not let it impede your dreams.

Now or Never

I have been a professional speaker for a long time. I started off talking about technology to people over 50. Then I spent a lot of time talking about sibling loss, which is great; I am still very dedicated to it. But talking about death all the time is tough, and I also want to reach a wider audience. I love speaking. And I have envisioned growing my speaking business, growing my audience, for seven years. I would speak at events and people would tell me I needed to get in front of bigger audiences, which was very encouraging. It is always great when someone else says, "You've got to do this," when you have never mentioned to them you aspire to do just that thing. However, even with my desire to do something and the outside encouragement, it still took me seven years to act. The cost of waiting was that I was living a lie. I was saying something that in my heart I knew was not true. And I did not like that; it was not a good feeling.

> *I believe that if we keep hearing something, it is because we are meant to do something about it.*

Time passes regardless of what you are doing. In my case, I was working on other things during those seven years. I went to graduate school and then I was doing my internship. As I was writing this book, I was preparing to take my LPCC licensing exam. Those things were important for me to do, and they gave me credibility as a motivational speaker and author. But regardless, I had to commit to work on my motivational speaking goal or I risked missing the opportunity and never achieving it. I believe that if we keep hearing something; it is because we are meant to do something about it. And I kept hearing from others this was something I should pursue.

> *Life is a participatory sport.*

If you do not take part in your own life, do absolutely nothing, life still goes on. **Life *is* a participatory sport,** and it is so much better if you actively take part in it, rather than sit on the sidelines and watch it pass you by. If you sit on the sidelines for too long, you risk missing or losing opportunities.

I know firsthand through the death of my sister that there is no guarantee of tomorrow. Not one of us knows what tomorrow brings, so do not put off the things that are important to you. You can lose your health, energy, and vitality as you age, so often later turns to never. Listen to the voice in your head whispering at you to "Go for it!" Listen to those people who keep telling you should do something and commit to getting started. It is now or never.

> *Later is always in front of you, but it never comes.*

Another reason to avoid putting things off is that the longer you do, the bigger and more difficult the task or goal becomes. One challenge many people faced during the COVID-19 pandemic is having too much time on their hands. I find when I have too much time it almost becomes more difficult to complete tasks. When I know I have hours of unscheduled time in front of me, it is easy to say, "I'll do that later."

However, later is always in front of us, but it never comes. And the task looms larger with every "later."

Ask yourself, are you taking part in your own life, or sitting on the sidelines? Are your fears stopping you from moving you forward? Is something else holding you back? If you do not go for it now, will you ever?

Know Your Value

When boldly proclaiming your intentions, you must stay true to your vision in every way. When we falter and question ourselves, the first thing we do is undervalue our idea, ourselves, or our abilities. Instead of saying, "I want to earn $1 million this year," we say, "I can't earn a million dollars. Who would pay me that much? Maybe I'll try for half a million."

Or I might have doubts and say, "I can't sell out an auditorium of 1,000 people, maybe I'll try a community theater that seats 200." If you never set the million-dollar goal, or I never set the 1,000-seats goal, we will never achieve them. **You can only reach the goals you set**. Maintain the value of your goal, whether that is pounds lost, miles run, books sold, seats filled, or dollars earned. Set your EPIC goal and keep your eye on the whole prize, not an undervalued portion of it.

> *If you have Ferrari ideas, do not sell them at go-kart prices.*

The Brownie Experiment

The Bevier Cafeteria at the University of Illinois conducted an experiment on what impact the presentation of food had on its perceived quality and value. They informed participants that the cafeteria was considering adding a brownie to their dessert menu, and they wanted to know what people thought of the brownie and how much they would pay for it.

They gave all 175 participants the identical brownie, except they presented them in three different ways. They presented one-third of the brownies on a china plate, one-third on a paper plate, and the one-third on a paper napkin. People who ate the brownie from

(continued on next page)

Understanding value is a lesson that will help you all the way through your journey. Have conviction in your plans and believe you can achieve your EPIC dream. When you have Ferrari ideas, do not sell them at go-kart prices. If you want a dollar and believe your idea is worth a dollar, then ask for a dollar, not a dime. When you excitedly present your idea to someone and tell them right away it is worth one dollar, why would they believe you if you waffle and start peeling the price all the way back to a dime as soon as they ask a question? **Know your value, be confident in that knowledge, and stick with it.**

Perceived value is also important. That is the value others see in what you are offering or doing. If you present your idea as valuable and with enthusiasm, then the perception of others is that it is valuable and a good idea. Marketing proves the concept of perceived value all the time. Designer clothes sell for 10 to 20 times more than those without a name brand label, even though the cost to make them is essentially the same. We believe an identical dish labeled differently to be better simply because the label says it is. The guy at the fair hawking vegetable slicers sells more, with his enthusiastic banter, than the silent vendor beside him selling high-quality chef knives. Why? Because the vegetable slicer guy's enthusiasm for his product makes people believe that nothing slices vegetables better, even though they have all happily been using a knife for years.

(continued from previous page)

a napkin described the brownie as "okay, but nothing special." Participants served the brownie on the paper plate said it was "good." But those who ate the brownie from the china plate not only described the brownie as excellent they also commented on the efforts being made to improve the cafeteria overall. The china plate group was also willing to pay more than twice the price for the brownie than those who ate from the napkin, $1.27 versus 53 cents. Participants served the brownie on a paper plate said they would pay 76 cents. People perceived the brownies presented in a more expensive way to be better and worth more, despite being identical to the other brownies.

How you package your idea and present yourself influences how others view it and you. So, make sure you present and value yourself how you want to be seen and valued.

Silicon Valley offers many examples of how being passionate about an idea and making bold proclamations of great things to come can raise huge investment dollars. Tech gurus, from Steve Jobs and Bill Gates to Mark Zuckerberg and Jack Dorsey, have been able to raise billions of dollars by making BIG, **bold** proclamations. If you tell people you are going to change the world and absolutely believe it, then people will believe you and buy into what you are saying. And getting them to do this is easier than you think.

Do not believe me? Look at the story of Elizabeth Holmes and her company Theranos. Holmes was a Stanford University dropout and only 19 years old when she came up with a revolutionary idea to use only a pinprick of blood, rather than the usual test tube in laboratory blood tests. Not only did Holmes not complete her university degree, she also did not have expertise in any of the key fields (medicine, science, blood testing, or advanced engineering) that she would need to rely on to develop her idea. Despite this, almost everyone Holmes pitched her idea to enthusiastically invested. And these were big name investors, doling out millions, even tens of millions of dollars: Venture capitalist Tim Draper, Oracle Corporation founder Larry Ellison, and media tycoon Rupert Murdoch among them. She also wooed high profile, powerful people to her Board including the former Wells Fargo CEO Richard Kovacevich, two former secretaries of state, Henry Kissinger and George Shultz, and former Secretary of Defense James Mattis. Holmes raised almost $700 million and at its peak the value of Theranos was $9 billion. All the investors claimed the primary reason they invested in Theranos was because of Holmes. They believed in her passion, her vision, and her drive. They bought into her enthusiasm for her project so much that they neglected to ask for audited financial statements or even proof of concept.

Sadly, in this case, Theranos was not everything Holmes claimed. In 2018, the Security Exchange Commission (SEC) charged Holmes, along with her former COO Ramesh Balwani with wire fraud. The SEC charges stated Holmes and Balwani raised, "more than $700 million from investors through an elaborate, years-long fraud." Both pleaded not guilty. The trial just started as we were about to publish this book.

Holmes's story is remarkable as both an inspiring example and a cautionary tale. It is proof that passionately proclaiming your vision with purpose has a lot of value; about $700 million worth! If a 19-year-old college dropout with no expertise in the arena into which she entered can raise $700 million by boldly proclaiming her intentions and dreams, then anyone can. Passion and enthusiasm are contagious! The caution here, however, is that you need to be careful not to buy into your shiny marketing pitch so heavily that you forget that to maintain integrity throughout your journey, you must have the goods to back up your claims.

Know Your Message

You can only boldly proclaim your intentions and dreams if you are clear. Develop an "elevator pitch" for your idea. Be passionate and enthusiastic when you make your proclamation. And be concise—in about a minute's time you need to articulate your vision.

I worked with several start-ups in the early 2000s. Some of these companies would take ten minutes to explain what it was they were doing, and it still was not clear. These companies did not survive. How can people buy into what you are selling if you are not clear about what you are selling? You must have a clear, interesting, concise, and emotionally engaging message. A story that people can connect to and helps them understand the value of getting on board.

When people ask me what I am up to, this is how I explain my journey:

"You know how people can be their own biggest dream killers? They think,

'I don't know where to start' or 'It's too late.' What I do is help people reclaim their hopes and dreams. As a speaker, I share my unbridled enthusiasm to reconnect the audience with their EPIC. All you need to do is start—as I share in my new book, *EPIC Begins With 1 Step Forward,* EPIC Choices create an EPIC Life!"

Part of knowing your message is understanding the difference between an intention, a goal, and a dream. I **intend** to grow the size of my public speaking audiences. My **goal,** though, is more specific, measurable, and tangible: by 2023 I want to be selling out auditoriums of at least 1,000 seats. My **dream** includes my intentions and goals, but it is so much more. It is BIG and **bold.** My vision exhilarates and excites me. It includes flying in private jets and being invited to speak on television and radio. My BIG dream is the fuel that keeps me energized throughout my journey.

Now it is your turn. What are your intentions, dreams, and goals? What does your EPIC look like?

"Nothing is impossible, the word itself says I'm possible."
Audrey Hepburn

EPIC ACTIONS

1. Enthusiastically proclaim your intentions to friends and family.
   - When you share what you are up to others cannot help but be excited with you.
2. Envision your BIG and **bold** dream and do not lose sight of it.
   - Keep your dream big. Do not water it down out of fear.
3. Know your value proposition.
   - Believe in your worth; do not undervalue yourself or your ideas.
4. Know your message—clearly and concisely.
   - Always be ready to sell your goal or dream with an emotionally engaging elevator pitch.
5. Visit www.EPICbeginsnow.com for more inspirational quotes!

CHAPTER 4

USE YOUR STRENGTHS TO YOUR ADVANTAGE

Lean into **your strengths!** Why? Because it is more positive, more fun, you will be more productive, and it allows you to strengthen your team by including experts in areas where you are weak.

Feel the Flow

When we enjoy what we are doing and lose track of time, it is a great feeling. Anytime we do something we are good at we enjoy doing it more. When we engage our natural talents, it shows. We get into a natural flow and whatever it is we are doing does not seem difficult or take much effort. It is those things, the things that engross you, that you should lean into throughout your EPIC journey.

For example, I do not think writing is a personal strength, but I could lean into my love for speaking to record a podcast and use that as a catalyst to write this book. Recording a podcast was new for me, but because I enjoy speaking it came naturally. I looked forward to my weekly podcast recording and planning sessions with Aurora, and the hour always flew by. I enjoyed every second of recording. I can say this about any opportunity I have to speak; I jump at it, grab the microphone, and am "on" the second my audience hits "play." I never hesitate, and never second-guess what I am going to say, nor my ability to say it. Never am I staring at the clock, wondering when it all ends. Quite the opposite, I forget about the clock. Once speaking, I lose track of time and new thoughts and things to say flow naturally from one to the next.

> 66   *You should spend at least 75% of your time in your areas of strength.*   99

We all understand this state. Musicians call it being "in the groove." Athletes say they are "in the zone." These are metaphors for what neuroscientists call "flow." The state of mind when we lose track of time and sense of self, and creativity and productivity elevate to their peak. Whatever puts you in this state is where you should focus your energy. You should spend at least 75% of your time in your areas of strength; ideally the ones that get you to flow state. You will have more fun along the way and be more productive.

Generate Positive Productivity

A 10-year study conducted by McKinsey & Co. found that CEOs were five-times more productive when in a flow state. The same researchers stated that if companies could increase the flow state of employees by 15 to 20%, overall productivity would double.

When I think about my own experiences, I do not find this study surprising. If you think about it, you probably do not either. When

The Neuroscience of Flow

Most of us have experienced the feeling of losing ourselves in a project or activity. In the 1970s, University of Chicago psychologist Mihaly Csikszentmihalyi was the first to coin this state as "flow." Author and flow researcher Steven Kotler defines flow as the "optimal state of consciousness where we feel our best and perform our best."

Over the last decade, scientists have discovered that there is a radical alteration in brain function when we are in a flow state. American University in Beirut neuroscientist Arne Dietrich describes it as an efficiency exchange where attention heightens, and we "trade energy usually used for higher cognitive functions for

(continued on next page)

(continued from previous page)

heightened attention and awareness." A team of neuroscientists at Bonn University in Germany also discovered that the pleasure-inducing hormones endorphin, norepinephrine, dopamine, anandamide, and serotonin kick in during flow. These hormones increase attention, pattern recognition, and lateral thinking, often considered the "three horsemen" of rapid-fire problem-solving. Major athletic achievements, scientific breakthroughs, and progress in the arts are all credited to flow. We perform at our peak when in this state.

you engage in something you love doing—painting, writing, running—you accomplish more and go further when you lose yourself, find your groove, or hit your stride. And what a feeling when you awaken from your trance, step back, and look with pride at what you achieved. The feeling of accomplishment is wonderful, but when you wrap your accomplishment in something you love doing, it is one of the best feelings in the world. Increased productivity is a significant reason to lean into your strengths, but if you are looking for more reasons, pride, joy, and achievement are feel-good justifications.

Share the Sunshine

Another reason to lean into your strengths is it opens an opportunity for someone else to take on other tasks and find their flow to your benefit!

Find your people. Besides accountability partners and cheerleaders, find experts to fill in the areas where you are weak. When you do this, you create a win-win-win scenario. You win because you are not wasting valuable time doing something you dislike or struggling to complete something at which you are no good. You also win because you are bringing someone onto your team who enjoys what they do and is good at it, so they will be very productive on your behalf. And the person you hire wins because they got hired to do what they enjoy, and they get to help you.

If you focus your time on the things you are best at and enjoy doing while sharing the rest of the workload with others who are experts in your weak areas, you will build a strong, productive support team.

Harness your Strengths

To lean into your strengths, you need to know what they are. We often know what we are good at, but not necessarily our specific strengths. I know I am good at public speaking, and I enjoy it. I spoke with adults from a young age, and it gave me confidence in my speaking abilities. But I did not understand why or how I was good at this, nor what other strengths went hand in hand with my speaking abilities.

Fortunately, there are tools out there to help us with self-discovery. An excellent tool for discovering your strengths is the Clifton Strengths Assessment (formerly the Clifton Strengths Finder). In my case, the test reported my top three strengths were Woo®, Communication®, and Maximizer®. According to Clifton, Woo means I like to "win others over." Strength in Communication speaks to my pleasure in explaining and describing things to others, hosting events, and speaking in public. Being a Maximizer reflects my desire to be the best at what I do and bring out the best in other people. When I learned these were my strengths, it was easy for me to connect the dots to my affinity for public speaking. I have never met a successful public speaker who had an inability to "Woo" their audience, could not communicate, and had no interest in bringing out the best in others.

Clifton Strengths Assessment

According to their website, the Clifton Strengths Assessment themes are "your talent DNA." They explain the ways you "most naturally think, feel, and behave." Their research studies have shown that people who know and use their strengths are more engaged at work, more productive in their roles, and are happier and healthier. The assessment comprises 177 questions and takes about an hour to complete. www.gallup .com/cliftonstrengths

The interesting thing here is that when I realized these strengths, I could reflect on the role they played in my life. I have always had an ability to get people to do things. Because of my ability to communicate and influence, I have been able to get things which I should not have been able to. An upgraded seat on an airplane, or an upgraded hotel room with a view. I recognize these occurrences result from my ability to communicate positively and "win others over." They respond by doing something for me. I am authentic in how I treat people, but I give them the opportunity to help me by asking if there is something they can do for me. If I am staying at a hotel and it is my anniversary, I ask if there is something they can do for the occasion. This simple question can lead to a room upgrade, a bottle of sparkling wine, or chocolate-covered strawberries. My strength of Woo plays a role here, but so, too, does understanding how and when to use it.

When I look at my top five strengths, Woo, Communication, Maximizer, Positivity and Activator, it all adds up to someone who sees the best in people, can get things done, and makes the people around me just as excited as I am. The funny thing is, I do this all without thinking about it. This is who I am.

The Clifton Strengths Assessment is one tool you can use to discover your strengths, but there are other ways to discover them. I encourage you to go find your strengths and do all you can to use them every day.

When discovering how to harness your strengths, the questions you should ask are not just what do you like doing and what are you good at, but what are your strengths and how and when is it best to apply them? You might enjoy running marathons and are good at it, but what makes you good at it? If marathon running is what you are good at, then your strengths likely include resilience, focus, and ability to pace yourself. Without these specific strengths, you would not be good at long-distance running. Now consider where you can use resilience, focus, and the ability to pace yourself in other areas to help you achieve your EPIC goals?

As important as it is to understand what you really love doing, it is just as important to recognize this is not always what you are best at. I enjoy running marathons, but I am not necessarily good at it. If completing them makes one a good marathon runner, then some might consider me good at it, but I have higher standards than that and so should you.

Doing things you enjoy is an important part of a balanced life, but the secret sauce to EPIC achievements is finding something you love, are good at, and that relies on your other innate strengths. Understanding what you are good at, including how and why, will go a long way to making you even better at it because you can harness those strengths to increase your productivity and creativity.

Acknowledge Your Awesomeness!

You are likely the meanest person in your own life. A flaw of human nature is that we are hard on ourselves. We say things to ourselves that we would never say to friends or family. For just a moment, reflect on the negative thoughts or feelings you have had about yourself in the last two days. How would you feel if your best friend said just one of those negative things to you? Probably devastated. SO WHY ARE YOU SAYING THEM TO YOURSELF? We overlook our strengths, under-value our contributions, and decline to acknowledge our achievements. For these reasons, we are terrible judges of ourselves.

To lean into your strengths, you must admit that you have them. **You are awesome,** you just need to remind yourself. Making a list of what you are good at will go a long way to helping you understand where and how you work best, as well as reinforcing your self-confidence.

Take some time to write a list of hobbies that you love, things that bring you joy, tasks that you completely lose yourself in, subjects you can talk about endlessly, and skills that you know you are good at. Examine the list for commonalities. Where do these things all intersect? It is that intersection point where you will find your sweet spot; the task and working environment that puts you in a natural flow state. That is where you will find the genuine power of leaning into your strengths.

In my case, the common thread was my desire to help people. That is what I am passionate about, and it gives me joy. Hearing my book on sibling loss helped someone was an inspiration to bring the message to more people. I love public speaking, but it is the desire to help people that propels me to pursue larger audiences. I know speaking is a strength. This knowledge gives me more confidence and I do completely lose myself when asked to speak. But I believe this makes me a better speaker. The audiences see and feel that I love what I am doing and that it comes naturally to me, so they cannot help but buy into my enthusiasm and passion. **Believing in yourself is key to others believing in you.**

Find Opportunities in Your Strengths

You might ask, "How do I lean into my strengths?" You recognize you are good at something, and that you enjoy doing it, but how do you harness it and use it to create opportunities? To get the answer to these questions, you need to ask yourself:

- Where can you use your strengths?
- Who can benefit from what you offer?

- What other things can you do that relate to your strengths that will bring you closer to achieving your EPIC goal?

When I wrote my first book about sibling loss, my known strengths helped me along the way. I knew I was an excellent communicator who had a positive outlook, which is a good start when talking about death. I also knew I had a story. And I believed others would benefit from a book about sibling loss. After I wrote the book, I recognized my message would reach more people if I used my innate talent as a public speaker to present its content to an audience. And after I started presenting the material to live audiences, I realized I could further use my talents as a positive communicator to help others as a grief counselor. Grief counseling led to me pursuing the LPCC. And all those things combined were necessary steps to achieving my EPIC goal of speaking before audiences of thousands.

Leaning into my strength as a speaker also led to recording the *EPIC Begins* podcast with Aurora, which initially was only about writing this book. But I discovered I love recording podcasts and interviewing people as it naturally ties in with my strengths. This led to me thinking about new content and continuing the *EPIC Begins* podcast on my own. I could have spent months, even years, sitting at my computer struggling to write this book in the traditional way. Instead, I leaned into my strengths as a speaker. I shifted the voice in my head saying writing another book is hard, to one that inspired me to write this book, and launch a podcast and a YouTube channel!

The lesson here is that once I knew my strengths, it was easy for me to see how those had influenced my career choices as a trainer, public speaker, writer, counselor, and podcaster. And each of these things naturally relates to the others, so they all benefit my EPIC goal.

Can you find a pattern like this in your life? What skills do you have and what have you already done that can serve your EPIC goal?

Embrace Who You Are

Once you have figured out what you love, what you are good at, and what your areas of strength are, embrace them all. Embrace who you are! I am bald, but I went bald intentionally before it happened naturally. I knew from genetics that I was likely to end up losing my hair, so instead of fighting it, I accepted it and shaved my head. My hair does not define me, and it is easier to maintain my bald head, so I embraced baldness. Now I do not think about it much.

We are all unique. We all react to things differently and have our own way of doing things. My way may not work for you, and your way may not be what is best for me. Approach your journey your way. If you are an early riser, do not beat yourself up for being tired by six o'clock in the evening. If you get energized at midnight, do not force yourself to sleep at ten. **Whatever increases your productivity and juices your creativity is the approach you should take to achieving your goals.**

"Accept yourself, your strengths, your weaknesses, your truths, and know what tools you have to fulfill your purpose."
STEVE MARABOLI

EPIC ACTIONS
1. Take the Clifton Strengths Finder Test.
   - Learning your strengths is worth the time and dollar investment!
2. Embrace who you are and how you work.
   - There is more than one way to do things, work in a way that is natural to you.
3. Make a list of tasks and/or hobbies that you lose yourself in.
   - Find the commonality in those things; this is where you will find where and how you work best.
4. Take advantage of the EPIC Action list found at www.EPICbeginsnow.com.

CHAPTER 5

READY, SET, NOT YET

WHEN PURSUING YOUR EPIC goal, there are going to be times when you think you are ready to go, but something happens that prevents you from taking the next step. That something might be your own procrastination or fears, a life event that throws you off course, or failure along your journey. When this happens, keep and present a positive attitude by replacing the word "no" with *"not yet."*

Seize a "Not Yet" Mindset

The phrase ***not yet*** is inherently optimistic and hopeful. It speaks to future opportunity as opposed to shutting down your dream. No is negative. Have you lost 20 pounds? No. Have you run a marathon? No. Have you completed your book? No. No is a dead end.

When you respond with "***not yet***" it lets people know you have not given up on your dream. It tells people you are still working on your goal, but simply have not achieved it yet. Have you lost 20 pounds? ***Not yet***. Have you run a marathon? ***Not yet***. Have you completed writing your book? ***Not yet***. It shields you from having to explain every step of your journey and how long things are taking. It is an open-ended response for you, one that keeps the doors to the future open while also allowing room for whatever life may throw at you.

There is also a tremendous amount of freedom in saying, "***not yet***." It gave me the freedom to create content for a podcast before I had an audience. If I waited for an audience, I would likely have been waiting for a long time. Instead, I said, the audience is not there yet, but I can develop the content and they will come. Not having an audience does not have to prevent me from taking steps toward my dream.

> ❝ ***Not yet*** *is a friend you should lean on throughout your journey.* ❞

Not yet is hopeful. It takes the pressure off having to have all the answers and allows you space to slow down, take things in, and thoughtfully consider your next step. For example, it is not the best time to make decisions when we are in crisis. Before moving on to the next step, we are better to wait until the crisis passes and we have a rational mind. *Not yet* is a friend you should lean on throughout your journey.

Keep Your Eye on the Future

When you seize the idea of *not yet*, you keep future opportunities open. In some ways, *not yet* also represents your list of EPIC goals and dreams. I have a *not yet* list. These are things I plan to do in the future but have not yet. I am *not yet* a best-selling author, nor have I yet to be a guest on a nationally syndicated talk show. I have *not yet* spoken to a stadium full of people, nor have I helped one million-plus people. I

The Power of Not Yet

There is scientific evidence to back up the benefits of adapting a *not yet* mentality. Stanford University Psychologist and author Carol Dweck has conducted research on people's personalities and how they link to success. In her book *Mindset: The New Psychology of Success,* she explains that people have one of two mindsets: a fixed mindset or a growth mindset. Those with a fixed mindset believe they are born with their talents and intelligence and there is little they can do to change these things. They link their success or failure to these unchangeable factors, which means they do not try again or try harder when they fail. In a 2014 Ted Talk, Dweck describes those

(continued on next page)

(continued from previous page)

with a fixed mindset as: "Instead of luxuriating in the power of yet, they were gripped in the tyranny of now."

Those with a growth mindset, however, believe that with hard work and effort, they can achieve anything. They have a *not yet* mentality. When they find something difficult, they do not give up, they say, they have not learned how yet. When they fail, they do not quit, they say I have not achieved it yet. Dweck found that when they taught this approach to school children, their achievement rates consistently improved.

also have not earned my pilot's license yet. By saying I have not done these things *yet,* I am keeping the possibility open to achieving them.

Saying **not yet** keeps not only your doors open but also empowers you by emphasizing choice rather than failure. When people ask if I am a best-selling author, if I answer with "no," it is a dead-end response. This also sounds like an admission of failure. I wrote a book, but I could not achieve best-seller status. I failed to become a best-selling author. However, responding with "**not yet**," tells them my books are selling, I am marketing and promoting my books, and that I do plan to be a best-selling author. It also buys me time. It says I am working on my goal, but I need to time to achieve it. I have not reached my destination yet, but I am on the road there.

Use "Not Yet" as a Shield

It is easy to let the words and criticism of others wound us so badly they stop us in our tracks. But you have a choice how you respond to people. You probably already choose to respond to people differently. If a stranger said they dislike your idea for a book, you likely would not care, but if your sister said the same thing, then you would start to hyperanalyze your choice and second-guess writing it.

 No one can make you feel bad without your permission. –Eleanor Roosevelt.

The question is, why react differently? We react differently because we give more weight to the opinions of people we respect and care about than we do strangers. But you can choose not to let those opinions make you feel bad, or the judgment of others make you feel like a failure. Eleanor Roosevelt famously said, "No one can make you feel bad without your permission." These are valuable words to remember along your journey.

You can use *not yet* to shield you from negative comments and people that cross your path. When you have BIG, **bold** dreams, people will question you along the way. It feels like a kick or an insult when someone asks if you have earned your first million dollars or sold 100,000 books. They know the answer before they ask. Admitting out loud that "no" you have not can make you feel like a failure. "*Not yet*" is a shield to their negative energy but also an opening to a conversation. It creates a window for them to ask questions about what you are up to and how things are going. And this gives you a chance to speak enthusiastically about your goals and dreams. **Talking to others creates opportunities for new connections and new ideas, and it gives energy to your EPIC journey.**

Be Patient

When you say *not yet,* you must accept and believe it. There will be times you have no choice but to say not yet. And there will be times you choose to say *not yet*. Good, bad, major, and minor occurrences can all disrupt your journey. Something might come along, like my choice to pursue my LPCC, that sends you on a detour. I did not give up on my dream to build my public speaking business. Instead, I patiently said, "*not yet*," while pursuing another goal.

> 66 *Success doesn't come overnight; it comes over time.* 99 –Zig Ziglar.

I would not have done either particularly well had I tried to do them simultaneously and I gain credibility as a public speaker with my new designation. Motivational speaker and author Zig Ziglar said, "Success doesn't come overnight, it comes over time." I was taking the time I needed to clear my slate so I could focus on my EPIC public speaking dream. I accepted temporarily, saying *not yet* to that goal until I was ready.

In accepting that I was saying *not yet,* I also had to believe it. I was not putting it on a list to do "later" for later to never come. It is my EPIC dream to help millions of people. I could not lose sight of that while working on other goals.

Not yet should not be a path to never. It is only a pit-stop. A rest station along the journey that allows you to check your engine, replenish your fuel, and adjust your EPIC dream to your detour. You are still on your way; you just have not arrived yet.

Go When You Are Ready

You can and should also lean on *not yet* during tough times. We all went through a hard time during the pandemic. Everything changed. Everyone was isolated, and the future was uncertain. Where I live in California, we also experienced devastating wildfires that left our skies looking like something from the apocalypse. Crazy perhaps, but it was during all this I embarked on my EPIC journey with this book and the *EPIC Begins* podcast.

I am dedicated to my dream, but I have had to pause and say *not yet* more than a few times. I was not getting outside and exercising as much I as like. This affected my energy levels. During the pandemic, the days were long, and it was easy to put things off. But I forgave myself for these setbacks. I looked outside and said, "*Not yet,* but when the skies clear." Or "*Not yet,* but when they lift the restrictions on gathering." It was much more optimistic and hopeful than, "I can't because of the smoke." Or "It's impossible because of COVID restrictions." *Not yet* **brings with it the promise of tomorrow.**

"I may not be there yet, but I am
closer than I was yesterday."
AUTHOR UNKNOWN

EPIC ACTIONS

1. Replace "no" with *"not yet."*
   - Not yet leaves the door open to still achieving your dream.
2. Make a *not yet* list.
   - If you write your dreams under the heading *not yet,* you put yourself on the hook to achieve them.
3. For ideas on how to be EPIC at any age, visit EPICbeginsnow.com.

CHAPTER 6

SETBACKS ARE PART OF LIFE

JOHN LENNON FAMOUSLY said, "Life is what happens when you're busy making other plans." Certainly, his wife and two sons experienced the truth of that statement in December 1980 when Lennon was shot dead on the doorstep of The Dakota where he lived. He had all kinds of plans at the time of his death. So, too, did his wife, Yoko Ono. Sadly, for the world, Lennon never got to pursue his plans. And Yoko Ono suddenly had to carry on with her life, facing the stark reality that even when you have plans, life happens, and they can change in a flash.

Unfortunately, that is life. Things happen all the time that throw us off course and send us spinning. I call these EPIC Unexpected events. None of us wants to prepare for death, divorce, bankruptcy, illness, accidents, or joblessness. If we are lucky, we will never experience some of these things; but others, like death, are a guarantee. EPIC Unexpected events can also be wonderful but still life-shifting, like getting married, having a baby, or earning a promotion.

Whether good or bad, as with everything else along your journey, you must prepare for and accept the unexpected. Also, remember to be kind to yourself if something unexpected sets you back. Setbacks can be opportunities to sit at the side of the road and take in the view until you are ready to start your journey again. And sometimes in these pauses, opportunities can arise.

Accept the Unexpected

On December 9, 1996, my older sister, Lucy, was murdered. This was an EPIC Unexpected event in my life. Of all the things I thought I might deal with in my life, murder was not one of them.

Lucy was a second-year student at UIC John Marshall Law School in Chicago. She usually left her apartment by seven in the morning. On that morning, a maintenance worker assumed she was not home, and broke in. But she was home studying for an exam. When he entered her apartment, she surprised him. He strangled her.

After he killed her, he jumped out her fourth-floor window to a second-floor roof, but the police apprehended him right away. There was never any doubt who killed her; they found the man with one of her monogrammed towels on him. He hanged himself 10 days later in the Cook County Jail, sparing my family and me what would have been a very public and painful trial.

My sister's murder was devastating. It was like being run over by a semitrailer-truck!

When my dad phoned and told me what happened, I remember I felt numb from the top of my head all the way down my body. I lived only seven miles from my parents, so I jumped in my car and headed straight to their home. But when I was in the car, I remember I got quite analytical about the things that needed to happen. I knew there was nothing worse that my parents could go through. I assumed they would be in such a terrible state I would have to take control of everything. As most children do, I underestimated the strength of my parents. Lucy's murder shattered them, but they managed what they needed to. Those first couple of days, though, were a blur. I have clear memories of talking to people and the conversations I had, but the world was mute, and everything was fuzzy.

We lost a good person that day, someone who had plans to help others. Lucy was a talented actor and singer and she loved both. She majored in theater at college but pursued law instead because she did not think she had the wherewithal to withstand the rejection and criticism that comes with a career as an actor. She wanted to be a district attorney or a public defender. A good choice, I thought, because I could totally see her using her theatrical skills to sway a judge or jury. She was a good example of someone leaning into her strengths and using her talent and passion in what probably would have been an effective way.

I started my healing process from her death when I had a moment of clarity on the Massachusetts turnpike in Brighton. I remember exactly where I was when I realized that I alone was going to have to figure out how to get through losing Lucy. Even though I had fabulous support from my family and friends, ultimately, I was the one who had to walk this journey. Someone else could not do it for me.

> " *Get busy living or get busy crying.* "

I also had a moment of insight about two months after Lucy's murder. I do not know why, or how I could do it, but I let go of asking, "Why did this happen?" I think it is common for people who are grieving to get stuck on constantly asking, "Why?" But it is a bottomless pit of a question because there is no answer.

It becomes a vicious circle that can prevent you from moving on for years, decades, or ever. Although it bothers me not to know why Lucy's murder happened and I would love the answer, I know I will not get that answer. It was liberating to stop asking the question. It took some weight off. I also had work to do on Lucy's behalf, which was keeping me a little busier, and that helped occupy my mind with other things. I realized that the only choice I had was to accept what had happened. I had to get busy living or get busy crying.

Lucy's murder changed me too. That EPIC Unexpected event in my life changed my career path and inspired my desire to help others. Through my pain and loss, I saw how I could help others, and in helping others, it helped me get through my sister's death. It led me to writing my book about sibling loss and doing the work I do with grieving siblings.

Pay Attention to Your Needs

Even before the idea for my book crystalized, I knew something was missing from the grief counseling field.

My parents knew many people in Boston. After Lucy died, I would bump into their friends and acquaintances, and they would always ask how my parents were doing. They would ask, and I would answer, but I realized no one ever asked **how I was**

doing. I thought that maybe my loss was less significant than my parents'. But our sibling relationships are usually the longest relationships in our life, and often our closest. When no one acknowledged my grief, it had a profound effect. I thought somehow my loss was not as important because I was *just* a sibling.

Whenever you experience an unexpected event, you need to pay attention to your own needs and listen to what your body is telling you. If you feel tired, rest. If you want quiet, seek it. If you need to talk, find an ear. If you need an outlet, get creative. If you feel depressed, get some exercise and sunshine. And if you feel sad, cry. Do not deny yourself your own feelings or berate yourself for feeling them.

It was important for me to express my grief and have it acknowledged and understood. It was something I needed to do to move forward with my own life. When grief goes unrecognized, it blocks people from healing. If others do not acknowledge your feelings, then you do not feel entitled to feel them. I went seeking help in books and elsewhere and quickly discovered that sibling loss was a neglected subject.

Be Open to New Opportunities

Had Lucy's murder not occurred and had I not suffered from the experience of losing her, I would never have ventured down the path of being an author.

Not only did I write *Making Lemonade: Choosing a Positive Pathway After Losing Your Sibling* about me losing Lucy, I wrote a second book called *Why Don't They Cry: Understanding Your Living Child's Grief* to help parents understand the Sibling Survivor™ experience. I never thought that I would write one book, never mind two books, and now this, the third.

> *Celebrate the rainbow that was your person's life.*

Sometimes when we are grieving, we resist moving forward or embracing new opportunities because we feel guilty, like we should not be enjoying life when a loved one has died or something tragic has occurred. But I believe we should celebrate the rainbow that was their life. Do not focus on the dot at the end. That is what I choose to do with Lucy. I celebrate her life that was, rather than carry around the weight of her murder. And, as a family, we did positive things in her memory, which helped tremendously.

One thing my family did was start a foundation in Lucy's name through which we have given to many charitable organizations. We also created a scholarship for a graduating attorney going into public service, because that is what Lucy was going to do. To date, we have given 23 Sprague Scholarships. We host dinner every year with our Sprague Scholars, and it is rewarding to see what they are doing and the positive impact that we are having through Lucy.

One of our recipients was in the military. When he entered law school, he learned many veterans were not collecting their entitled benefits. Often the veterans did not even try to apply because the paperwork was too confusing. Our scholar started a veteran's law clinic in Chicago to help this important population in the area. After graduation, he served in the Judge Advocate General's (JAG) corp. The clinic is still running and helping scores of veterans access their much-needed benefits.

It is a lot more rewarding to do positive things in Lucy's memory than to be bitter and focus on her murder and why it happened.

Choose a Positive Pathway

I am a big believer in choice. One of my favorite mottos is, "Choosing a Positive Pathway™." Choice is one of the most powerful tools we have. When faced with EPIC Unexpected events that knock us off our feet, it is good to remember that you get to choose how to react. And the choice you make will determine your healing and health. When grieving a loss, there are many stages we go through. Some of those stages are naturally more grueling, heart-wrenching, and negative than others, but you can choose how you respond and what impact the event has on you and your life.

By Choosing a Positive Pathway™, I am not forgetting or ignoring what happened to my sister but choosing to celebrate the time I had with her. Lucy's murder happened when she was 30 years old. That means I got to spend 28 years with her. There are so many stories and memories that make me smile. We shared a lot of fun times together and my life is richer when I remember those happy times. And I am not bitter about what happened because I get to celebrate Lucy and I do great things in her name.

Death is not the only form of loss. Loss is loss. Losing your job, the end of a relationship, health problems that affect your quality of life are just some losses we experience. When we go through these things, we often feel alone and isolated. But know you are not. Besides your circle of friends and family, there are also organizations, therapists, and books to help you heal and carry on.

Every new day presents you with choices. What you choose to do and how you choose to view what happened is all up to you. Seek support, look for things to celebrate, find things that make you feel light and hopeful, and trust that things will get easier.

Optimism Helps

During troublesome times we are often told "think positive." It turns out this advice might not be as trite as it sounds. American psychologist Martin Seligman conducted research that found optimists view setbacks as temporary and changeable. It showed that by teaching people to think like optimists, it might be possible to immunize them against learned helplessness, depression, anxiety, and giving up after failure.

Delay Decisions

Avoid big decisions and be kind to yourself in the aftermath of an EPIC Unexpected event. You need restoration. Treat yourself and take care of yourself. For example, one of the most stressful things we can go through is losing a job. We tie much of our identity to our work, not to mention our financial well-being, so our self-confidence and security are rocked when we find ourselves unemployed. But this is one of the best times to take a vacation. You have time and it gives you the opportunity to lick your wounds and clear your head.

Once you have reset with a little self-nurturing, then ask yourself the questions you need to turn your EPIC Unexpected into EPIC Opportunity. Assess what you liked and did not like about your job? What were you good at and what did you really enjoy doing? Do not get stuck in the trap of: "This is what I do, so this is what I always must do." **Change can be scary, but with change comes growth and opportunity**.

You can apply these same questions to any EPIC Unexpected event, bad or good. Say you lost your house in a fire. Your family is all safe, but the home is a write-off. After self-nurturing and allowing yourself time to accept what has happened, you can then ask what you liked and did not like about the house. How do you want your new home to look? How can you make it better, environmentally friendly, and energy efficient? Losing your home in a fire would be a shocking EPIC Unexpected, but it presents an opportunity to build a better home and create memories in it.

The same practice should apply to unexpected but good events. Newlyweds, for example, are best to wait a few months after getting married before making big life decisions. Not that getting married is exactly unexpected but love usually comes into our lives unexpectedly and marriage can come quickly. Meeting "the one" can change all your plans in an instant. But it is not a good idea to make major life decisions in the days right after your wedding. Give yourself time to absorb the celebration and the new relationship dynamic. Celebrate and nurture the new beginning. Then, after a little while, consider what you want your new life to look like and where you would like to go next.

Regardless of what the EPIC Unexpected event is in your life, avoid making major decisions when you feel overwhelmed.

Reflect

When you face a loss, this can be a good time to reflect. Life has presented you with change, whether you wanted it or not. You may have had little or no control over the loss, but you have control over how you respond.

During the pandemic, there was a lot of loss: jobs, businesses, relationships, and lives. With so much uncertainty surrounding us for such a long time, it was easy to get stuck in a hopeless loop of "Why me?" and "Why now?" But why is not a helpful question. Instead, when you are ready, ask yourself questions that will help you not only survive your EPIC Unexpected event, but also eventually thrive.

- What is good about this situation?
- How can I view this occurrence as an unexpected growth opportunity?
- Who can I help and who can help me?

This comes back to the **97/3 Rule** again. I do not think people stick with things they think are crap, not relationships and not jobs. So even when these things end, we should be able to look back and find more positive than negative. There must be things about the job that you enjoyed doing, or that you felt successful at, just as there must have been things about your relationship that brought you joy. Focus your energy on those things. Spending your time thinking and talking about all the bad things will only give the bad things more power and energy. When thinking about and planning for your future, nurture the things that make you feel good.

Not that you should completely ignore the bad things. It is always important to assess honestly the role you play in your own life. Do not fall into the trap of thinking things happen to you. Remember, **life is a participatory sport!** So be honest with yourself about your participation and the impact it had on your current situation.

If, for example, you lost your job or your marriage ended, ask yourself:

- How did you contribute to the demise?
- If you could do things differently, would you?
- What would you do differently?
- How can you use these insights in your next job or relationship?

You should also pay attention to any self-destructive behaviors you might have developed.

- Are you addicted to drama or toxic relationships?
- Has that addiction led to a pattern of seeking employers and relationships that feed the addiction?
- How can you meet your needs in a constructive (rather than self-destructive) way?

This should not be an exercise in self-loathing, but one of self-discovery. If you answer these questions honestly, then you will find yourself in a more emotionally intelligent place when planning for your future.

Control Your Thoughts

Frequently, we are our own worst enemy. When things go bad, we are exceptionally good at talking ourselves into a worse place. Using the pandemic as an example, isolation took its toll. As weeks dragged into months and the national death toll rose, it was easy to convince ourselves that things would never improve. The economy would never bounce back, and joblessness was going to carry on into the unforeseeable future. It did not take long to spiral into a dreary place.

When this happens, the best way to reverse the spin is to ask yourself: "Is that really true? Where's the evidence?" "What proof do you have things will never improve?" "What proof do you have you will not find another (better) job?" Shut down the negative chatter with things you know, instead of feeding it with things you do not.

Listen to Your Body

When facing setbacks, it is also important to listen to your brain and your body and consider the impact one is having on the other. We are much more critical of ourselves than we are of others. And we are good at hyperfocusing on what we think are our flaws or failings. What we are not good at is determining the impact our overall well-being has on our decision-making abilities.

For example, there might be a certain time of day when you feel tired and irritable. When feeling like this, it is not a good time for you to check progress on your measurable milestones because you will focus on those you have missed and leave yourself feeling unsuccessful and frustrated. It is best to check your progress when you are feeling upbeat and energized, so you are more able to approach the list with a "***not yet***" attitude, rather than a "I failed" one.

> *"When dealing with a loss, focus on the rainbow that was that person's life, and not the black dot that marks the end."*
> ZANDER SPRAGUE

EPIC ACTIONS

1. Get Exercise.
   - Exercise will help break the cycle of depression.
2. Breathe.
   - Consciously stop and take deep breaths and remind yourself things will get easier.
3. Find a creative way to express your grief.
   - Do something you have always wanted to do, like paint, learn to play an instrument, or take a dance class.
4. Reconnect with your friends.
   - Even if you have not talked in a while, rekindle old friendships.
   - Amazing things happen when we reconnect with people.
5. Check out www.EPICbeginsnow.com to find resources to help you through life's setbacks.

CHAPTER 7

FAILING DOES NOT MEAN YOU ARE A FAILURE

ALONG YOUR EPIC JOURNEY you are going to fail. I am not saying this to be discouraging, but to prepare you. From the outset, you need to shift your mindset from "if" I fail, to "when" I fail. Be prepared for the inevitable. No one is 100 percent successful all the time. Some failures are just little missteps or stumbles, but some can be much more catastrophic. Regardless, it is best to view failures as unavoidable life lessons. **Only those who have never tried anything new can claim to have never failed.**

Prepare for Failure

Hope for the best—but prepare for the worst. Insurance policies are based on this theory. No one purchases home, vehicle, or life insurance hoping they will have to use it. We buy insurance hoping we NEVER have to use it. But should tragedy occur, it buffers us from the worst consequences.

Preparation for failure will minimize long-term consequences. The sinking of the Titanic was a disaster. Had the engineers considered the possibility of hitting an iceberg, they could have averted tragedy. Over 1,500 people lost their lives on April 15, 1912, when the "unsinkable" Titanic sank. Do not be like the Titanic, so confident in your superiority that you believe yourself to be unsinkable. Paradoxically, considering what could go wrong can prevent problems.

Preparation will also empower you to pivot and recover. If you are prepared for the storm, it is easier to weather. When things go wrong, do not beat up yourself. Negative self-talk will not change what happened and it will not help you move forward from it. Keep your eye on your big goal and do not become discouraged when things do not go as planned.

Define Failure

Just as we must define success for ourselves, it also helps to define failure. If you know what failure looks like to you, you can think about ways to avoid it. For example, if I talked about writing this book but never did anything to make it happen, then that would be a failure.

Defining failure makes you look at your big goal from a different angle and forces you to ask big questions:

- What does failure look like to you?
- What impact will minor failures versus enormous failures have on your goal?
- Is the bar by which you measure failure realistic?
- What are you going to do when you fail?

When I first set my marathon goal, if I had said, "If I cannot run 26.2 miles within one month, then I will have failed," then I would have failed! It takes a plan, time, and dedication for a runner to achieve marathon distance. If I set an unrealistic goal for myself from the outset, then I would have done nothing but set myself up for failure. Instead, I set measurable milestones that I could check off as successes throughout the journey. How can you apply this milestone method to your goals?

You must set realistically achievable goals. Failure for me means never speaking to over 100 people. I cannot, however, expect to sell out a stadium within a week of publishing this book. If that is what I expected, then I am guaranteeing failure for myself. Instead, I must attach a realistic deadline to my goals and decide along the way when to say, "I need help," when to say, "***Not yet,***" and when to accept that I did, indeed, fail and then ask, "What next?"

To reach my goal of helping millions of people, I must first start by speaking to dozens, then hundreds, then thousands, and then tens of thousands of people. I will not jump from 0 people in the audience to 10,000 overnight. I can, however, set a goal of selling out 6 events with 100 audience members by a specific deadline and then work toward that milestone. Then if I do not achieve it, I can assess from there. However, whether I achieve that milestone, my big goal remains intact.

Missing a milestone does not mean you failed to achieve your EPIC. You only missed a step.

When considering possible failure points, be sure not to exaggerate missteps and miscalculations as catastrophic failures. When I first started writing this book, I wanted to release it by Spring 2021. But it took longer than expected to write, so it was not released until February 2022. Miscalculating how long it would take to write and missing my self-imposed deadline was not a catastrophic failure. It did not end the project, nor did it derail me from my EPIC speaking goals. It simply delayed my release date. The rest of my EPIC goal and plan to achieve it remained intact.

Once you have defined failure, and differentiated between missteps and catastrophic errors, consider where you might fail and what you can do to mitigate it. Prepare for likely setbacks—have a backup plan. Doing this might help prevent the failure altogether.

Look for Lessons in Failure

Einstein said, "Insanity is doing the same thing over and over and expecting different results." When you deny your failures, you not only risk going crazy, but you also waste energy, time, and money trying the same thing repeatedly. And you miss the opportunity to learn.

We have all heard the expression: "When one door closes, another opens." Well, there is some truth in that. We put all our efforts into something but never find the success we are hoping for, so we define this as failure, a closing door. But perhaps these are not failures but messages that we should open a different door to new opportunities. When we fail, it does not mean we should quit, but that we need to stop doing the same thing over and over and try a fresh approach.

Consider my past career as a trainer in the tech industry. I found that I have a knack for learning new software and then turning around and teaching it to others. It is a unique skill set that I used to my advantage in the job market. Before applying for training jobs, I would research the company and confirm they were solid, had staff, and had money to pay me. But trainers are always the last to be hired when things are good and the first to be fired when things go bad. So, I lost many jobs, although no one used the word "fired." They outsourced me, downsized, reassigned, whatever they wanted to call it, but I was changing jobs a lot.

Losing a job is not a good feeling, and it does not make you feel like a winner. This sad cycle of researching employers, starting new jobs, losing the job, only to start all over again got old for me. I asked myself: "Why am I teaching someone else's material?" I knew I had a ton of great material that I would much rather teach. This realization led to grad school and ultimately this EPIC journey. My "failure" working for others led me to seek a better fit for myself. If I had more success as a trainer working for others, I might never have realized I wanted to present my material to a much broader audience and likely never would have pursued venturing out on my own.

What lessons can you find in your failures? Where is there a hidden opportunity?

Feed Success Not Failure

When you fail, do not wallow in it. Do not keep a list of missteps or tally of tumbles. Hockey players take dozens of shots at the net during a game, but the only ones they count are the ones that score. All professional athletes track their achievements this way. In baseball, a lifetime batting average of over .300 is excellent. Think about that. It is a player's job to hit the ball, and we consider them the top of their field if they do this successfully only 30 percent of the time. This means they fail 70 percent of the time they go up to bat! But that is not what they count. No one says they have a negative 700 batting average; that would sound terrible. Imagine how much better you would feel about yourself if you were content with a 30 percent success rate.

Intelligent Failure

In a 1992 article entitled, *"Learning Through Failure: The Strategy of Small Losses,"* Duke University professor of management Sim Sitkin talks about "intelligent failure." He presents the idea that intelligent failures are a crucial step in organizational learning. Not all failures classify as intelligent. Sitkin says a failure must meet five criteria to qualify as intelligent failure:

1. The failure resulted from something that was thought out and planned for.

2. The failure was unpredictable— you had no way of knowing in advance what the outcome would be.

(continued on next page)

(continued from previous page)

3. The failure is modest and manageable, not catastrophic.

4. The failure is dealt with quickly, so there is no lost time between outcome and lesson.

5. The lesson learned does not exist in a silo, it must relate to the bigger picture or organization.

When viewing failure through the lens of learning, it can reveal weaknesses, show where time or money is being wasted, and expose where ideas are being held onto stubbornly. Intelligent failure leads to smart lessons.

This goes back to the **97/3 Rule**. Do not put too much energy and thought into the 3 percent of things that do not go well. If you spend the afternoon picnicking and it rains for 10 minutes out of the entire afternoon, do not make the day about how the rain ruined the picnic. Most of the day was pleasant, and you got to enjoy the company of others in a lovely environment. Why would you want to focus on the ten minutes of rain? Focus on what went right. Count your wins and celebrate them. And take the losses, learn what you can from them (check the weather forecast before heading out for a picnic) and then move on.

When you fail, it is best to adapt a growth mindset and the *"**not yet**"* attitude discussed previously. Failure does not mean you should give up and quit.

Failure does not mean you are not capable of success. And failure does not mean you should never try again.

When you fail, it is an opportunity to learn. It gives you a chance to step back and assess where you are and what you should do next.

- Was it a failure or a miscalculation?
- Why did you fail?
- How did you fail?
- What does this failure mean?
- How will this failure impact your journey and goal?

The answers to these questions will provide you with the information you need to best adapt and shift course.

> *I have not failed 10,000 times—I've successfully found 10,000 ways that will not work.* –Thomas Edison.

Know the Difference Between Failure and Fraud

When you are on your EPIC journey, it is important that you believe in yourself and present your goal or dream with enthusiasm, but it is equally important to be honest with yourself. Be careful not to buy into your own sales pitch so much that you forget to back it up with action and results. When you deny your failures, you cross the line into being dishonest with yourself and others. If you do not admit when you have failed, you risk becoming a fraud.

Elizabeth Holmes and her company Theranos are a good example of making this mistake. Holmes had to believe 100 percent in her blood-testing machine Edison to raise the funds she did and grow Theranos into a $9 billion company. She also had to convince investors and board members that she was making progress with its development. Without progress, investors question their investment. Instead of admitting to investors that development was taking longer than expected, she was secretive about development, while exaggerating the success she was having. In doing so, she trapped herself. The more she raved about how well Edison worked, the more interest grew in it. Eventually she signed a deal to put Edison machines in Walgreens across the United States, even though it appears she was aware the machines could not do what she claimed they could. The Walgreens deal ultimately exposed the truth about Edison. Instead of admitting temporary failure, Holmes oversold herself to where she could not deliver, making herself look like a fraud.

None of us likes to admit when we have failed. Failure is not a good feeling and does little to boost our confidence. But when you have failed, it is important to admit it because you cannot learn from your failures nor find opportunities in them if you never acknowledge them. Had Holmes been more forthright about the challenges she was having, and where she was having them, she might have been able to find an expert or partner to help her over the hurdle. Edison is a great idea, and it is easy to understand why investors and those working in medicine would be excited about it. Honesty might have bought her more time, and she might be closer today to achieving her dream. Instead Theranos dissolved, and Holmes is facing trial for fraud.

Do Not Let Fear of Failure Stop You

The higher you set your bar, the more likely you are to fail along the way. If you never fail, you have likely lowered your bar and competitive field. Do not lower your bar out of fear of failure. If you are seeking to be the best at whatever you are endeavoring to do, then you will fail in the beginning. You are still learning. There are people out there that are better than you, have been doing it longer, and who have applied the lessons of their failures to get where they are. If they are who you are trying to reach or

Presidential Failure

President Abraham Lincoln is an excellent example of someone who persevered through great tragedy and failure. In 1832, he was defeated in his run for the Illinois State Assembly. In 1835 his sweetheart died. He suffered a nervous breakdown in 1836. In 1843, he lost the nomination for the U.S. House of Representatives. He lost renomination in 1848. And in 1854 and 1858 he was defeated for U.S. Senator. He did not give up though, and in the end achieved what some would consider the greatest accomplishment of all when he was elected President of the United States of America in 1860.

surpass, then they are your competition. Accept that in the early days of your journey, they have the competitive advantage, so you may fail by comparison.

For example, say you want to win an Academy Award as a director. Steven Spielberg is your idol. You plug along directing small indie films until finally The Academy of Motion Picture Arts and Sciences nominates you for an OSCAR®. But you are up against Spielberg, who ultimately wins. So, you lost. You failed to win the Academy Award. You must accept this failure. But, in this moment of failure, remember that you would not have lost had you not tried to place yourself in Spielberg's company to begin with. So, had you not tried, you would not have failed, but that would not have counted as a win either.

> " *Failing does not mean you are a failure, but a champion at trying.* "

Do not let fear of failure prevent you from trying. In life, we usually connect our biggest regrets to the things we did not do or try. At the end of our time on this earth, we are far more inclined to ask, "What if I had?" as opposed to "What if I had not?"

"What if I had asked that person out on a date?"

"What if I had written that book?"

"What if I had traveled to Egypt to see the pyramids?"

"What if I had lost 50 pounds?"

If you allow fear of failure to dictate your choices, you will be asking, "What if I had?" at the end of your life. If you choose to go for it, in your last days you will probably say, "Wasn't that awesome that I tried?" and "Wow, look at what I achieved." So, face potential failure with the knowledge that failing does not mean *you are* a failure, but a champion at trying.

"If you want to succeed, double your failure rate."
TOM WATSON, CEO, IBM

EPIC ACTIONS

1. Think about what failure looks like to you—what would you consider failure points?
   - Make these realistic; do not set yourself up for failure by setting impossible goals.
2. Think about how you can mitigate those potential failures.
   - What can you do to prepare in advance to prevent the failure?
3. Look for the opportunity to learn from failures.
   - View failures as lessons you can apply to future endeavors.
4. Embrace the Mistake.
   - No one is perfect. We all make mistakes.
   - View your mistakes as growth opportunities.
5. Visit EPICbeginsnow.com to link to the EPIC Begins podcast and hear stories of EPIC failures turned into EPIC success!

CHAPTER 8

PLANNING YOUR EPIC DREAM

AN EPIC JOURNEY requires a structured plan. In the previous chapters, I worked to shift your mindset to prepare you for your journey. You have a BIG, **bold** dream you are excited about. You are ready to share it with the world. You believe in your dream and yourself. You are revved up and ready. But everything talked about up to this point is just that, talk. A healthy mindset is important, but without a plan and a structured approach to tackling it, you will not get far.

Write Your Plan

This is an oft repeated piece of advice: *Write it down*! If you are forgetful, *Write it down*. If you have a lot of tasks to complete: *Write them down.* If you have a goal you want to achieve: *Write it down.* Why is this piece of advice given so often? Because it works. It is amazing how much more real things become when we write them. When we declare our goals in writing, we become accountable to ourselves. It is difficult to read plans and goals you have written and committed to doing—but then, day after day, be confronted by your lack of meaningful progress.

    66   *Remember, your plan is not your goal.*   99

Write what you want to achieve and your plan for achieving it. Remember, your plan is not your goal. I bring this back to running marathons. My goal was to run a marathon. My plan to achieve this was to get up every morning and train until I could run 26.2 miles.

Think about the steps you need to take to achieve your goal. You probably do not know all the steps that you will need to take, but you likely know some. I know some steps I need to take to prepare to speak in front of thousands of people around the world, but I do not know all of them. That is okay though. I can work on what I know; the other things will come to light as I progress. You can also start working on what you know, and your pieces will come to light.

My EPIC journey to earn my LPCC is a good example of this. I knew broadly what I needed to do: attend graduate school, earn my master's degree, intern, and take the licensing exam. I did not know what the process would look like. I did not know how graduate school would go. And I did not know where my internship was going to be. But I did not need to know any of those things to start. Once accepted to graduate school, I figured out how to study and the other steps necessary to complete the degree fell into place. I did not know each step beforehand but keeping my eye on the big goal guided my way.

When developing your plan, also make sure it includes feasible steps that you can accomplish and control. Often, we think we have failed at something because we include steps that are beyond our control, and, therefore, unachievable. But we did not fail, we set the wrong goals. If, for example, I want to get 100 online book reviews within a month of publishing this book; I do not really have much control over that. I can, however, take what I know and apply that to steps I can control. I know about 1 in 100 people will write a review of a book they have read online. This means that to get 100 reviews, I need 10,000 people to read my book. Now the question becomes, how do I get my newly released book to 10,000 readers within a month? A little digging revealed that I can give away free advance copies of the book on several e-book platforms. So now the plan is not to "get 100 reviews," which I cannot control, but to give access to 10,000 free advance copies, something I can control.

What can you control along your journey?

When you first write your plan, it is only a preliminary plan. It is your initial road map, but not the exact route you will take to your destination. As you progress along your journey, your plans might change. You will discover things. You will come across detours that present new opportunities. And you will face some roadblocks. You should expect to adapt and add to your plan as you go. One key to succeeding through your journey is your willingness and ability to adapt and pivot as things change.

Develop a Timeline

Once you have written a rough plan, attach a time line to it. Start at the end with your vision of your achieved goal and work backward from there.

My end point for earning my LPCC was passing the exam. I had not been in formal schooling for 22 years, so embarking on the journey was scary. I knew it would not be a quick process, so I tackled it like my pizza. I sliced it up into manageable pieces. I felt ill-prepared to return to formal education after so long. I knew I had to get my studying muscles back into shape. My first milestone was to pass the first semester. When I achieved this, it was easier to believe I could carry on. A fun fact is that I did the best I ever had in my academic career because I was studying psychology and counseling, and these subjects fascinate me. This made studying and succeeding easy.

By setting short milestones throughout your longer journey it also presents opportunities to celebrate achievements along the way. It is best to recognize your hard work and reward yourself throughout your journey. It would have been a long, difficult six years if I waited to celebrate until I had earned my LPCC. Instead, when I passed the first semester, I rewarded myself with a pair of headphones. It felt great to buy them as recognition for my accomplishment; it was piling on the joy of my achievement. I repeated this method over the six years. When along the way there is no pleasure in achieving your EPIC goal or dream, it is more difficult to stick with it in the long run. And, if there is no joy in doing it, what is the point?

When we can see the finish line, it is easier to believe we can reach it. Sometimes, though, the finish line is too far to see. If your EPIC goal is so huge the end is out of sight, build in measurable milestones along your journey you can check off and celebrate. And use these milestones as a guide to keep you on track, motivated, and focused on your EPIC dream.

Why Vision Boards Work

Dr. Tara Swart is a neuroscientist, medical doctor, author, and a vision board expert; although she prefers to call them action boards. She explained her thinking in *Forbes* magazine saying, "Action boards are the new vision boards because making a collage then sitting on your porch waiting for the checks to roll in is a fantasy." Dr. Swart believes instead in using neuroscience to achieve your dreams. The goal with your action board is to create something that inspires you to manifest your dreams through your actions. She says vision or action boards, if used correctly, are effective for several reasons. Our brains use value-tagging to process information and to keep the important stuff and filter out the rest.

(continued on next page)

Create a Vision Board

A vision board is poster board collage of pictures and quotes that have meaning to you. It works as visual motivation and inspiration. I cut out pictures from magazines or type up and print out words or phrases that inspire me. I hang my vision board above my desk so when I am working, I can look up at it to draw motivation from it and reaffirm the things I have proclaimed.

When creating your vision board, go BIG! My vision board does not include photos of me carrying my luggage into a motel, because this is not my dream. Instead, it includes a picture of a private jet because I envision a need to travel easily from speaking engagement to speaking engagement. It also includes photos of beautiful travel destinations, because travel is a reward that I plan to give myself as I achieve my goals. I think there are powers hidden in vision boards. They are a lot of fun to create and a helpful thing to do to get and stay motivated. What BIG, **bold** things would you add to your vision board to inspire you?

Share Your Plan

Tell people about your plans. When you tell people about what you are planning, you are now accountable to those people. If I tell people I am writing another book, when I see them, they will ask me how the book is coming along. I better have made some progress, or I look foolish.

Including "active" members on your team, people who are involved and invested, helps with accountability. An exercise partner is

(continued from previous page)

Our brains give higher value to images than written words. The more we look at the images on a vision board, the higher they move up in importance in our subconscious.

Because the brain cannot differentiate between an experience and a strongly imagined vision, we can trick it by feeling like what it is like to have already achieved our dream. But it is also important to envision the work it is going to take to reach your goal. Research has shown it hinders results when you only visualize the results and not the steps to get there. Finally, Dr. Swart notes that our bodies naturally fear new things. When you look at the same images repeatedly, the brain no longer registers them as new, so the natural stress reactions ease, reducing the feelings of fear attached to achieving your goal.

a good example of an active accountability partner. It is easy to say, "I am going to exercise every morning." It is not so simple to do when you wake up, your bed is warm, and the room is cold. Talking yourself into staying in bed is easy. But if you know your friend is waiting for you at the park, you get up and go meet them. You involved them in your exercise regime, and they are counting on you to show up. If they were not waiting, you would be more likely to stay in bed.

When you share your plan, you also reaffirm your belief in yourself. You are telling others you have a plan, but you are also telling yourself. Every time you say your plan out loud, it becomes more real. And the more real it becomes, the easier it is to tune out the negative voices in your head, as well as the wet blankets in your life that keep insisting you "can't."

This is important, so I am repeating it: choose your people wisely. When sharing your plans and dreams, be sure to share them with people who are going to be supportive and enthusiastic. When we doubt ourselves, we reinforce our negative thoughts by talking to people who agree with our negative viewpoint. If, for example, your brother rarely says anything kind about your driving, he is probably not the fellow to tell your dream is to become a race car driver. If, however, you had a driving instructor who said you have a natural affinity for driving, tell him! Avoid the people who say "can't." You might not succeed at everything you try, but you will learn something either way. Believe in your plan, share it with enthusiasm, and move forward with confidence.

When you share your plan, you also open the doors to opportunities. Ask other people what they do. When you do, they usually ask about you, and this gives you the chance to share your plans. You could discover they can help you, or that you might be able to help them. Do not be shy. If you never share your plan, then it remains a secret and it, along with new connections and opportunities, remains behind closed doors.

If you do not share your plan, you also miss the chance to receive valuable feedback and insights. It is easy to develop blind spots when analyzing our own plans. We need to be our own cheerleader, so sometimes we cheer right through things we should not. My dream might be to have 200 speaking engagements a year, but if I share this goal with someone who has had to travel 200+ days a year, they might caution me about the challenges with this kind of demanding travel schedule. They can offer insight that I did not have, which gives me the opportunity to revise as I see fit.

When receiving feedback, be careful not to give more credence to the negative comments than positive ones. Most of us are guilty of this, including me. After a speaking engagement, I can have a dozen people come up to me and tell me how much they enjoyed it or how much I helped them. That is a great feeling. But one person might say, "Gee, I really can't relate to that," and that is what I obsess about.

I was speaking at a conference about understanding your living child's grief and lots of parents came up and thanked me for the information. One parent, whose loss was very recent, came up and said that I did not understand her pain, and I was wrong. What do you think I remember about that presentation? Initially, it was that one parent, but then I kept reminding myself that so many had liked it, and that this parent was perhaps not ready to take in the information I shared.

It is not realistic for me to expect to wow 100 percent of the audience. But I am human! I must tell myself the same thing I am telling you, which is to consider the 3% negative feedback and whether there is something to learn from it. But avoid focusing on it too much because it will only drag you down. Believe the 97% positive feedback. You can even type it out and add it to your vision board. It will be the wind behind your back that propels you toward your dream.

Refine as You Go

> *The result of things not going as expected is feedback, not failure.*

This is an important point: refine your plan as you go. For example, nobody sits down and writes a perfect manuscript for the first time. A book goes through several drafts before it goes to an editor, a fact checker, and then a proofreader before it is ready for publication.

Approach your EPIC plan the same way. Work on the plan in front of you but be open to improving your plan along the way. You are going to try some things that do not work out as anticipated. If you maintain your **not yet** mindset, then the result of things not going as expected is feedback, not failure.

You need to be ready, willing, and able to pivot. Do not be stubborn with an idea when it is clear it is not working. Something might sound like a good idea in theory, but in practice, it does not quite work out. Then accept this and refine your plan.

Things can also happen that you have no control over. In my case, it was the pandemic. In February 2020, I attended an event hosted by my longstanding friend and mentor, Aurora Winter. I left pumped about embarking on my EPIC journey to build my public speaking business. I had visions of speaking at full stadiums across the country. A month later, we were in lockdown. It did not matter how much I visualized myself standing in front of a stadium full of people, I could not manifest that while a pandemic was gripping the globe. So, I had to pivot.

People were at home more. They had more time on their hands and were looking for different things to occupy their time. YouTube Channel! Podcast! That was the pivot. I redirected my focus to writing this book and sharing its content through online platforms. Which potentially introduces me to a much wider audience than I could get traveling around the country. I still wanted to increase my speaking engagements because live audiences are my wheelhouse. But until I could, I continued to work on my EPIC dream through different avenues.

How can you pivot to create new opportunities?

Revisit Your Plan

If you want to stay on track and reach your goal, then you must tend to your plan. Do not neglect it. It is not good enough to write your plan once and then never look at it or revise it again.

Check in on your plan every couple of months, asking these questions:

- Are you on track?
- Is there anything you have forgotten or missed?
- Are there things that are no longer relevant?
- Does your timeline need to change?
- Do you need to find someone to add to your team?

I had to adjust my plan several times while writing this book and building my speaking business. Pandemic news and restrictions changed daily while Aurora and I were recording podcasts and creating the content for this book. It was impossible for me to work on some aspects of my plan until I knew when businesses would reopen, and government would allow group gatherings. Due to this uncertainty, I had to move the steps related to large public speaking engagements to the ***not yet*** list.

Writing the book also took longer than expected. Preparing for taking the LPCC exam took me away from this project for a while. And then when I returned to it, I decided I needed an editor to help get it from podcast transcript to a cleaner manuscript, but finding the right person was difficult. But, with Aurora's help, we found the perfect editor, Racquel Foran, who has done a great job. So instead of my book coming out in the spring of 2021, I released it in early 2022.

When revising your plan, do not make the mistake of rushing at the end. Often the last leg of the journey is the longest—but the most important. A pro basketball game is a good example of this. The clock might say there are only two minutes left in the game, but it takes ten minutes to play that two. The players cannot pack up and leave the court after five minutes, even if they think they have the game in hand. They must play out the clock to celebrate their win, so must you.

When you revisit your plan, you learn where you need to revise and pivot and ensure you are implementing your complete plan to keep your EPIC journey on track and your EPIC dream alive.

"Plans are nothing, planning is everything."
Dwight D. Eisenhower

EPIC ACTIONS
1. Write what you want to achieve.
   - What are the steps that you need to do to achieve that goal?
   - What is the preliminary plan?
   - Who do you need to help you achieve it?
2. Create a timeline for achieving your goals.
   - Start at the end and then work your way back to where you are now.
   - Create short-term milestones along the way that you check off and celebrate.
3. Create a vison board that represents your EPIC goal or dream.
   - Cut out pictures and words that have meaning to you and hang the board where you will see it every day.
4. Share your plan with positive people in your life and ask people to be your accountability partners.
   - Believe unfailingly in yourself.
5. Refine as you go.
   - Reframe failure as feedback.
   - Pivot if you need to.
   - Revisit the plan every few months to see where you are.

CHAPTER 9

ACHIEVING YOUR EPIC DREAM

EVERYTHING IN THIS BOOK up to this point has been about helping you shift your mindset from an "I can't" attitude to a "Just watch me!" one. You have learned how to find and use your strengths. You have discovered what brings you joy. You have been shown how to use those things to create opportunities and momentum for your journey. You have been taught the benefits of resilience through setbacks and failures. And now you feel ready to proclaim your intentions and dreams to others. But I am sure you have asked many times, "But **how** do I achieve my dream?"

Over the course of your journey, you will probably never stop asking how. It is impossible to know every outcome before we begin, so how will be a common question. Right up to the point when you achieve your dream and then ask, "How did I do that?!"

Although you might not have the answer to every "How…?" there are specific actions you can take that will increase your chances of a sipping a glass of champagne celebrating your achievement while asking, "How did I do that?"

Break Down Your Plan

I know you want the whole pizza. You have been dreaming about the whole pizza. You crave every morsel of that big, delicious pie. But it is not possible to shove the entire thing into your mouth all at once. The outcome of attempting to do so would be disastrous. I can say the same for achieving your EPIC goal or dream. You cannot approach it all at once. You need to tackle it in small, manageable pieces.

Spend some time thinking about the steps you need to take to get to where you want to be. When doing so, also think about the order things need to happen. And I do mean "think" because you do not know. You might think things should proceed in a certain order, but as you progress along your journey, additional information comes to light, and this can change the order. So, **think about the steps and their order, but understand things might change.**

There will be many steps that you know you must take to achieve your EPIC goal. I knew I had to write this book to have a book to promote. I also knew that there were certain steps I had to take in the publishing process, like hire an editor, design the cover, and write the back cover text. I could not publish this book until I had all its pieces pulled together. Writing a book is a huge EPIC goal that feels overwhelming but by breaking down the process into manageable steps—record the *EPIC Begins* podcast; transcribe the podcast; edit the transcription into book format; design a cover; write cover text, etc.—no one step seemed too big.

What are the big steps you need to take? How can you break down your big goal into more manageable steps?

Remember, when breaking down your plan, it is possible to work on two parts of the plan parallel to each other. I am not talking about multitasking, (e.g., doing two things at the same time, but two or more things being able to occur concurrently.) For example, your EPIC dream may be to travel to East Asia. This is an expensive trip, and you will need to save a lot of money. But it will also require a lot of research to ensure you enjoy your experience. It is easy for you to do your research and plan where you would like to go and how to get there, while also saving money for the trip. There is no need to wait to do the research until you have already saved the money. **When making your list, consider which smaller steps you can check off while working on bigger ones in the background**.

Make a Schedule and Stick to It!

When thinking about the steps you need to take to achieve your EPIC goal, include scheduling. You are much more inclined to tackle the things on your to do list if you have it scheduled into your day. I am a big fan of structure and schedules are key to structuring your days.

> *Save the whipping cream to the end.*

I learned at a young age the only way I could succeed academically was with structure. From grade four on, I approached homework in a very scheduled and structured way. I always started with the subjects I liked least, and worked toward my favorite subject: math, English, history, science, and then Latin. I enjoyed everything about Latin. It did not feel like studying when I was learning this; it was something to look forward to. If math was my broccoli, then Latin was the whipping cream on my dessert. I knew that if I left my least favorite subject to the last, I would never get it done. By starting with the thing that I found most difficult and liked the least, I was working on it when I had the most energy but also saving the whipping cream to the end.

This approach has great psychological impact, too, because as you check off each task on your schedule, you know that the next task is going to be more enjoyable, and so on. It motivates forward momentum. Imagine if you were on a treasure hunt and the first prize found was a diamond, but when you found it, they informed you that each subsequent prize would not be as good as the previous one. How motivated would you be to continue deciphering clues and hunting if you had already found the best prize? Now reverse the scenario. The first prize was a silver ring, but you were told each subsequent prize would be better than the previous. Now how motivated would you be to carry on with the treasure hunt? Clearly, we are all going to be motivated by the proverbial carrot dangling before us, more than the dirt we pulled it from, so start with the dirt and work toward the carrot, not the other way around.

When you schedule your time and structure how you use it, it also helps ensure you allot enough time to complete the things you need to do and makes sure you use the time wisely. I relied on a structured schedule for managing my academic studies all the way through to completing my LCPP and the system never failed me.

I also used this method when writing this book and developing everything involved with *EPIC Begins*. I created a schedule for myself to manage planning how I was building *EPIC Begins with 1 Step Forward*. I scheduled time for creative brainstorming, writing, creating videos, researching what tools I might need to help me do my job, and meeting with the people on my team. **How do you need to adjust your daily, weekly, or monthly schedule to accommodate your EPIC goal?**

When working on your EPIC plan, starting with the thing that is most difficult, have regularly scheduled specific, realistic time slots to work on the tasks. Block off regular weekly meetings with people on your team, as I did with Aurora, to create ongoing momentum. Usually, the things that require the most focus and attention are best done first. For me, editing the *EPIC Begins* podcast was a difficult, time-consuming task. It was something that I did best in the morning when I was feeling fresh, and my patience was high. If I left editing until tired at the end of my day, I would become much more frustrated with the finicky, repetitive work and it would take longer, and I would not do as good a job. So, I learned to set aside 90 minutes first thing in the morning two days after we recorded each session for editing. This got the task done and off my plate, so I was free to move on to things I enjoyed doing more.

What tasks are best for you to tackle when you are feeling fresh and energetic?

When developing your schedule, also remember to plan breaks. Depending on the duration of your task, your break can be as small as standing up and doing a series of stretches to a full-hour lunch break, but regardless of duration breaks are important. It always helps to step away from what you are working on to allow your body and brain an opportunity to rest and refresh. Sometimes a few minutes away from a task can give you a whole new perspective when you return to it. Taking a break helps prevent task fatigue and frustration from setting in.

Tackling tasks or activities at the same time of day, in the same logical sequence, starting with the most difficult thing and saving the things you like doing to the end, will keep you on a steady, productive course to your destination.

Outsource

I am a fan of outsourcing. Why do for yourself what you are not that good at, when you can get an expert to do it for you? There are many things you can do for yourself, but it is not necessarily the best or most productive use of your time. For example, I outsourced editing my books. I could edit them myself, but it would take me longer than an expert and I would not do as good a job. Hiring someone to do it is money well spent. It frees me up to do other things that I am better at, and I also get a better book faster by hiring someone else to do that work.

We often fall into the trap of doing things ourselves because we "can," and because we think we will save money, but there are a lot of ways to measure value beyond money. Sometimes it is worth it to spend a little more because you get better results. Revisiting that EPIC trip to East Asia, you can spend your time searching travel websites and reading online reviews of destinations to plan your own trip. And you might even plan a decent trip. But if you invest in a travel agent or tour operator who is an expert in East Asia, you are much more likely to get the experience you are looking for. An expert will not make the mistake of booking you in 2-star hotel, if you are looking for a 5-star hotel, but you might! Here, hiring an expert can eliminate a lot of worry and stress when you are on the trip. A worthwhile investment, I think.

Avoid falling into the trap of saying, "When I'm successful, I will hire someone to help me." If financially possible, outsource to experts whenever you can. You did not begin this EPIC journey so you could spend all your time toiling away at things you do not enjoy and are not good at. If you spend your time doing this, you will become discouraged. When you outsource to experts, you are building a team of people who are invested in your success. They can act as mentors. Not only will they save you time and do a better job than you could, but they are also people to whom you become accountable. They can cheer with you when you succeed and talk and encourage you through struggles.

Where can you outsource? Is there something you do not enjoy doing, an area you need support, or a task you are not good at? If there is, then find someone to add to your team who can help you!

Set Measurable Milestones

Setting measurable milestones along your journey is a key step in keeping you motivated to carry on. If all you do is work but see no actual progress or reasons to celebrate, it is tough to maintain enthusiasm. A sense of accomplishment is one of the most rewarding feelings we have. You are more likely to achieve your goal if you find pleasure along the way. Having measurable milestones will keep you on track. Celebrating them will infuse your journey with pleasure.

When you work hard to reach an achievement, reward yourself. You deserve a prize. Several years ago, I began a weight loss journey. I set weight goals over a period of months. I wanted to lose 10 pounds in the first two months–when I achieved that goal; I rewarded myself with a bottle of expensive but delicious Monkey 47 gin. The goal was to lose 25 pounds. When I did that, I rewarded myself with a shopping spree—none of my clothes fit after all. When I was craving dessert, I thought about a sharp blazer I had my eye on and it was easier to skip the sweet treat.

The reward system has always worked to motivate me. Knowing there is a prize at the end of my effort is a huge psychological boost. When I was in school, there were three honor rolls: third, second, and first. My parents set out different rewards for making these honor rolls. I think they understood my abilities and knew that I would not achieve the 95% average required to make first honor roll, so the reward was a mini dirt bike. I never got that minibike, but man, the thought of that potential kept me working hard. I made third honor roll for the first time in 6th grade and the reward for that achievement was a new stereo. This thrilled me! I loved that my hard work paid off.

Is there something you covet you can use to reward yourself along your journey?

Keep Your Eye on the Prize

Once you have proclaimed your dream, keep your eye on the prize. You know what you want, believe you can get it, and be steadfast in your determination! Do not talk yourself out of your dream because it is difficult, or you met a roadblock, faced a setback, or it seems like it is taking too long. Accept what comes your way, be willing to pivot, and open to different roads to your destination.

It is common for all of us to fall into the comfort of routine; doing things the way we always have because it works and there was nothing to force us to change. This does not mean that this is the best way to do things, or the best route to take. It is just the comfortable habit we have fallen into. Sometimes forced detours, even if they delay our journey, can introduce us to a more pleasant, if not faster, route.

I used to work for Intel. It was an hour commute each way to work for me. From the first day, I figured out the "best" (e.g., fastest) route to get there and back. And for years, day after day, that is the route I took. It never even occurred to me to seek a different route. Why should I? I had already figured out that this was the best route. And then one day there were dual accidents along my usual route that forced traffic to detour. The detour took about ten minutes longer than my usual route, but it was a much more beautiful drive. I remember thinking, "Why have I never gone this way before?" Of course, I knew the answer. I was comfortably set in my ways. However, once I learned of that alternative route, I had a choice each day. If speed was the priority, I stuck with my old route. But sometimes I was in the mood for the alternate route because it made me feel good. The journey was a little less stressful and a lot more pleasant.

Set your eye on your destination and do not waiver from it. Plan your journey and prepare for as many things as you can. Also, consider whether you are stuck in a comfortable routine and if you might benefit from changing things up a little. Not all detours are unexpected, some are planned, either way, do not resist them.

You must also be relentless in your quest. This goes back to not listening to the naysayers in your head, or the wet blankets in your life. You must never take your eye off the prize while in pursuit of your dream, regardless of insecurities or the irrelevant opinion of others. People will tell you that there are things you cannot do. You might even say this to yourself. Do not believe it! You can achieve your dream if you are always thinking about and working on ways to do so.

I had a dream to travel to Australia. From the time I was a boy, the place fascinated me, and I was determined that one day I was going to visit. I started dreaming about this when I was in grade school. Obviously, I would not achieve that dream then. But I held onto it. I never lost sight of my dream to go to Australia and I was always looking for opportunities to make it happen.

My dream came true in college. I wanted to spend a semester in Australia. The school I attended did not have a program there, so I had to find a program in Australia and convince my school to let me attend. I was both a psychology and history major. One requirement for a history major was that we had to take at least one course about three different continents. Most people did the Americas, Asia, and Europe. But knowing that Australia is a continent and a country, I said I wanted to take Australian history. I also knew my school did not offer Australian history, so I suggested I go to Australia to finish the requirements for my degree. I gave them academic justification for me to go to Australia and they agreed. It was fascinating! I learned so much and the experience shaped who I became. But it all happened because I never gave up on my dream and was relentless in my pursuit of it.

Never lose sight of your goal or dream; if you envision it, you can make it happen.

Share Your Achievements

There is nothing more boring than celebrating alone. If you pop a champagne cork and there are no friends there to hear it, is it any fun? I do not think so. Share your achievements with others when you are excited and happy. Others cannot help but get excited right along with you. It also feels good to hear praise, receive validation, and get recognition from others. When I passed the LCPP exam, I shared this achievement on Facebook, and the comments and feedback I received were wonderful, especially during a pandemic when I could not celebrate face-to-face with people. Who do you want to share your success with?

> *When things get difficult, encouragement can be your life vest.*

I used a trick when I was training to run a marathon. I had a T-shirt printed with my name on the front. Then when I was out running, I would pass strangers and they would yell out, "Yes! You got it, Zander!" It was outstanding. It is powerful to get that kind of inspiration when you are slogging along. When things get difficult, encouragement can be your life vest.

When I was in fifth grade, I went from a school where I had two hours of homework a week to having two hours of homework a night. My parents referred to that as the year of tears. I cried so much; it was hard because I was a slow reader and there was a lot more reading. But my mom and my dad were encouraging. We worked out ways for me to do it. For example, I might have to read 15 pages a night. That would take me forever! So, my parents developed a system where I would read a page, my mom or dad would read a page, and then I would read the next, and so on. And that encouragement and belief in me helped me through that challenging time.

Seek people who will encourage you and who you can share your achievements with. When you doubt yourself, encouragement will help you over the hump. When you reach an achievement, having someone to celebrate with will make it more fun!

Be Your #1 Cheerleader

If you do not believe in yourself, then how can you expect others to believe in you? If you are not enthusiastic, then why would other people be? Be both kind and encouraging to yourself. Remember the *97/3 Rule.* When things go wrong, do not focus on the 3% that was bad. Instead, encourage yourself by saying out loud to yourself the things you would say to a friend or family member to encourage them. It is amazing when we speak out loud to ourselves how impactful it can be. Tell yourself out loud that you are doing great! That you have got this! Cheer yourself on to push yourself beyond your own expectations.

Think about exercise classes here. The workout is hard. You are doing it, but every move is torture. The instructor keeps asking you to do more difficult things. In that moment, you say to yourself: "Okay, just one minute more. It's only one minute! I got this, even though I feel like I'm one heartbeat away from collapse." But with that self-encouragement, the minute passed, and you made it. You might feel you are out of steam and wonder how you are going to continue, but if you just keep encouraging yourself, you will make it to the next step.

In those moments **when you are asking yourself: "How do I do this?" Answer with: "I already am!"** How do I, Zander, write a book? I already am! How do I record a podcast? I already am! How do I become an award-winning international speaker? I already am on that journey!

How do you lose 20 pounds? You have already started! How do you earn a degree? You are already working on it! How do you become the best in your field? You are already training to do so!

Achieving your EPIC dream comes down to breaking down your plan into pieces, developing a structured schedule with measurable milestones, rewarding yourself when you reach those milestones, shouting your successes from the rooftops, and when you ask yourself: "How do I do this?" Answer: "I already am!"

> *"Start where you are. Use what you have. Do what you can."*
> Arthur Ashe

EPIC ACTIONS

1. Break your plan down into bite-size pieces.
   - Understand the order that you think things need to happen.
   - Ask yourself: "What can I do in parallel?"
2. Outsource where and what you can.
   - Ask yourself: "What are the tasks that you can outsource?"
   - Invest in others who are experts in the areas you are not.
   - Find a mentor to help you.
3. Set milestones to measure your progress.
   - The journey is easier when you have waypoints to aim for along the way.
   - When you reach your waypoints, reward yourself.
4. Keep your eyes on the prize.
   - Be open to more than one path to reaching your goal.
   - Be relentless in your drive to achieve your dream.
5. Share your progress.
   - Praise is motivating, so share your good news and success.
   - When life is tough encouragement can be your life vest.
6. Be your #1 Cheerleader.
   - If you believe in yourself, others will believe in you.
   - When you find yourself asking, "How do I?" Answer with: "I Already Am!"

CHAPTER 10

ENJOYING YOUR EPIC JOURNEY

THIS IS IMPORTANT to remember: enjoy the journey! Whatever your EPIC goal or dream is, I am sure you did not set out to achieve it through misery. There will be challenges along the way, and times when you doubt yourself, but do not lose your joy when these things happen.

Be Present in the Moment

In your determination to achieve your EPIC goal, do not focus so intently on the pot of gold that you forget to enjoy all the colors of the rainbow. Remember to slow down and pay attention to everything around you. Stop to smell the roses, notice the view, and feel the warmth of the sun. Do not go through your journey with blinders on to everything else. When you live in the moment, you are more likely to discover new things, meet new people, and embark on fresh adventures because you have left yourself open to these opportunities.

" *Don't forget to look around often.* "

When I spent my college semester in Australia, I also traveled to New Zealand. Because I was young and an adrenaline junkie, my focus at the time was getting to Queenstown so I could go bungee jumping. All I cared about was getting from Christchurch to Queenstown. But New Zealand is a gorgeous country. I would have been a fool to not absorb and enjoy everything the landscape offered. One stop along the way was Fox Glacier, which is in Westland Tai Poutini National Park on the West Coast of New Zealand's South Island. It is a spectacular place. I took photos, but they could not capture the grandeur of the place. I, however, am forever grateful that I took the time to look up and look around instead of keeping my head down and focused only on my goal of bungee jumping. The photos may not have done the place justice, but I will hold the memory of seeing that glacier for the rest of my life. If you want to enjoy your journey and get the most out of it, do not forget to look around often.

Reflect on How Far You Have Come

When looking around, make sure you do not spend all your time looking ahead. It is just as important to look back and reflect on what you have accomplished and how far you have come. This relates to setting measurable milestones that you can celebrate along the way. Some journeys can take years to achieve. If you spend all your time focusing on what you still must do, it will rob you of acknowledging what you have done.

The best analogy I can think of here is mountain hiking. Most mountain hikes have a summit destination that offers a spectacular view. That view is the reward for the hike. But the hike might take hours. If you spent the entire time with your head down, focused only on making it to that last destination, think about everything you would miss along the way. Yes, your aim is to reach that million-dollar view, but your hike will be more enjoyable if along the way you stop and pick some berries, drink some water while taking in the view of where you already traveled, and listen to the birds sing from the branches above.

If you are feeling frustrated because you still need to lose another 10 pounds, be kind to yourself and remember that you have already lost 15! Look at a photo from three months earlier and compare how you look. Reflect on the time, energy, commitment, and effort it took to lose those 15 pounds. Tell yourself how great you look. Enjoy what you have accomplished so far.

If you are training to run a marathon, throughout the training process, reflect on the progress you have already made. Remember when you could not run around the block and be proud of the fact that you can now run to the park and enjoy the surroundings while you are running. Do not downplay your progress.

Sometimes it is difficult to see you are moving forward because it is taking a long time to get to your destination. When this happens, stop, and note where you started, then compare that to where you are and acknowledge how far you have come.

Tell Your Story

Your journey will be so much more fun if you share it with other people. And you never know what might transpire when you share your dreams with others.

I have been fortunate to have traveled to many places. Part of the fun of traveling is getting to share with others the places that I have visited. And sometimes this motivates those people to add that location to their bucket list. This happened with a good friend of mine from high school. We loved the Crosby, Stills, and Nash song *Southern Cross*. When I went to Australia, I took a picture of the Southern Cross.

I told my friend I had seen it and that he should see it sometime. That put the seed in his mind that he wanted to see it too. So, he traveled to Australia and many years later admitted he made that effort because he did not want to miss out on seeing the Southern Cross. Sharing my experience with him inspired him to seek the same experience.

I also encourage you to share your EPIC journey with new people. You never know what might come from a conversation. I kept rediscovering this when sharing my EPIC journey of writing this book and creating the *EPIC Begins* program. Every time I shared what I was doing, I discovered new people that I wanted to interview about their perspective on EPIC journeys. This would not have happened if I had not shared what I was doing with others.

When I meet new people, I also get curious about what they are doing. They may be on their own EPIC journey and perhaps they have had no one to share it with. When you open conversation and show enthusiasm for what others are doing, it is contagious. They will share enthusiastically what they are up to but will also be more curious about what you are up to. You never know what opportunity might arise from sharing your dreams.

You can also share this book with others. If you know someone who is also embarking on an EPIC journey, you could become accountability partners and use this book together as a tool to guide you through your journeys. Or you could start a mastermind group and focus on one chapter a week of the book to motivate each other to continue moving forward on your journey. Having this kind of encouraging support can go a long way to inspiring you to take even bigger EPIC steps.

Connect and engage. Find new communities of like-minded people. If you cannot find one, create one. I did! The aim with this book and the *EPIC Begins* podcast is to encourage people to take that first step toward EPIC. Providing a supportive community environment where people on EPIC journeys can hear stories about how others are doing on their journey, share their challenges, and celebrate their successes is key to meeting my EPIC goal of helping millions. With this in mind, I launched EPICbeginsnow.com. This is the place where those who read this book and listen to the *EPIC Begins* podcast can connect and support each other.

Share your journey, share your enthusiasm, encourage others to share theirs, and then watch the momentum of your EPIC dream build. And if you are looking for people to share with, are struggling to get started, or need help to stay motivated, then EPICbeginsnow.com is there to help guide you through your journey.

Roll with the Detours

This is worth repeating: Detours are part of the journey. Roll with them! When there is construction on the highway or an accident that causes a detour, there is nothing you can do about it. It would be ridiculous for you to sit in your car on that blocked road, honking your horn and raging for someone to open the road. You could sit there all day, but nothing would change except you would likely have a headache, sore throat, and would be late for wherever it was you were going to. The reasonable thing to do is accept what has happened and take the detour. You know that by doing so, you will still make it to your destination, and if you are lucky, you might benefit from the new route. There is nothing to be gained from resisting and complaining about detours. This will only slow you down.

Sometimes the detour we find ourselves on is of our own making. We make a mistake or ask the wrong question and suddenly find ourselves on an unexpected path, but even then, we must accept the situation. There is nothing gained by endlessly bemoaning an error. I learned this the hard way when I was a boy. I was on a summer school trip to the Pacific Northwest. We drove from Boston. On the way home, we stopped in the Black Hills of South Dakota, where we went on a walk. We could choose how far we wanted to go; I, along with three other boys, chose a seven-mile walk. We set out on our journey. A little way into the walk, we came to a fork in the road, and we did not know which way to go. There was a house there, so I rang the bell to ask for help. I asked the owner, "Does this road to go to Rochford?" And she answered, "Yes, it does." So, we set off down the road I had asked about.

Now this was a hard lesson in asking the correct question because, although the road took us to our destination, the journey was 14 miles, not 7. The woman answered the question I asked, but I did not get the information I was looking for. What I really wanted to know was what was the shortest route to our destination, because clearly both roads took us there. None of us were happy about doubling the length of our walk, but there was nothing to be gained from complaining. The detour happened. It was less than ideal, but we still made it our destination and we survived to take on our next adventure.

Detours are a part of life that we experience all the time: when driving, when traveling, when planning our lives. When faced with a detour, it is up to you how you choose to react to it. The detour is happening whether you like it or not, but you can choose to make the best of it. Roll with the road you are on, seek the surprising delights along the way, and be open to what is around the bend.

Push Outside Your Comfort Zone

When pursuing your EPIC goal or dream, it is not the time to play it safe. You will not achieve EPIC if you do not push yourself to be EPIC! Before you take your first step toward EPIC, you must believe you can take that step and every single step that is required, no matter how difficult, how scary, or how impossible it might seem. When you face your fears and believe in yourself, the profound effect will amaze you.

When I was in college, I spent 48 hours alone on an island in Penobscot Bay, Maine, as part of the Outward Bound program. The reason I joined this program is that I had always been uncomfortable being alone. I wanted to face this fear. What better way to do that than by spending two days alone on an island? I remember when I was there; I found a comfortable rock by the water. I sat on it with sun beating down on me, listening to the waves; it was one of the few times in my life where I could say I was in a meditative trance. I processed and worked through so many things that I had pushed down. When I came out of it, I felt a weight had been lifted from my shoulders. I felt much better and more confident with having worked through some issues I had about being alone. I was better after having faced my fear.

Another experience that I was fortunate to have was to go on safari in Africa. My friend, who is a safari guide, suggested we camp out on one of the safari platforms. The platforms are in place for rangers. They keep you safe from the more dangerous predators like lions, but there are plenty of animals like baboons that could still make their way up there. I was not keen on the idea. We had an expensive hotel room with a comfortable bed. Why would I want to sleep on a platform in the bush? I had my daughters with me, though, and they were keen to do it, so I agreed.

I admit it scared me when the idea was first presented, but I am so glad I did not let that fear dictate my choice. What an experience it was! I did not know, but the bush is quiet at night. The animals that you know are there are silent. I had an excellent sleep and I have a lifelong memory to share with my daughters.

Are your fears holding you back? Do not let them. Push yourself, even if it is uncomfortable to do so. It is in the discomfort that you will discover your true strengths and how brave you are.

Pushing yourself outside your comfort zone also requires lifelong learning. If you decide you have learned everything you need to, then you are unlikely to push yourself. But there is always more to learn, and the more you learn, the more you grow. And the more you grow, the more you want to learn!

You are never too old to pursue a postsecondary or postgraduate degree. I was 45 when I returned to grad school. But learning does not just mean pursuing a formal education. Read, talk to people, watch documentaries, visit museums, try new things, and share what you know and have learned with others. It is fun to tell people: "Hey, I'm trying to learn this." Learning new things keeps your brain elastic, and you engaged and excited about your life.

Help Others

We consider it selfless to help others. I think it is selfish, though, but in a good way. We benefit exponentially when we help others. Helping people feels good. Sharing what you know with others makes your learning feel more worthwhile. Giving your time to those in need takes the focus off you and your troubles. There is no downside to helping others.

For me, knowledge does not hold the same value unless shared with others. Imagine if Edison had invented the light bulb but told no one! I have always enjoyed sharing my knowledge with people.

I grew up on a tree farm. We grew white oak on 18 acres of land. Every spring break, I had the "fun" job of stacking seven-and-a-half cords of wood that we would then use throughout the next winter in our woodburning stove to heat the house. One year in school, we had to do oral presentations on a chosen subject. I did my presentation on tree farming. It was fun for me because I got to share all this stuff that I knew other kids did not. I got to share my living experience with them and teach them something new. It was so cool!

Then there is the compassionate, human side of helping that is extremely rewarding. My family founded the Charisma Fund in honor of my sister, and through that charitable fund we have done amazing, fun, meaningful things in Lucy's memory. This has not only helped us through our grief journey, but also many others through theirs. I mentioned in a previous chapter the law school scholarship we started in Lucy's name. While writing this book, I was reviewing applications for it and was so inspired by the passion and dedication of these young legal scholars. We have donated to charities that do important work and to outdoor schools in Northern California that bring children from inner cities who have never seen the ocean, beach, or forest to spend a week exploring and learning about nature. To alchemize the grief of Lucy's death into something good is magical. It feels good to do good.

Be Happy!

Finally, do not forget to smile, even, or perhaps especially, through the tough times. I know it sounds silly, but believe it or not, forcing that frown upside down can affect your state of mind. You reflect what you project. Remember why you are doing what you are, remind yourself of how far you have come, enjoy the journey, and smile.

"Two roads diverged in a wood and I — I took the one less traveled by, and that has made all the difference."

Robert Frost

EPIC ACTIONS

1. Pay attention to what is around you.
   - Be present in the moment and seek opportunities.
2. Share your progress with others.
   - Stories, achievements, and celebrations are more fun when we share with others.
3. Roll with the detours.
   - Detours are part of any journey. Do not resist what you cannot control.
4. Push yourself outside of your comfort zone.
   - Face your fears, challenge yourself, and never stop learning.
   - When we learn, we grow. And when we grow, we want to learn more.
5. Help Others.
   - It feels good and does good—win, win!!
6. Share your success with the EPIC community at www.EPICbeginsnow.com.

REVIEW AND WRAP

ONGRATULATIONS! You have reached the end of this book, demonstrating your persistence and commitment. You should now be ready to plan, achieve, and enjoy your EPIC journey.

At the beginning of this book, I told you that pursuing your EPIC goal is as simple as taking one step forward. I also told you it was easy. I do not want to undervalue the importance of your goal, or how difficult it is to commit to and stick with the actions required to achieve your goals and dreams. But **taking one step is easy.** Just one step. Do not even think about how far it is to your destination, just take a step toward it. As soon as you take one step, you will find it is easier to take the next. Your momentum will build.

All journeys begin with the first step. The first step will feel difficult before you take it but remember you can simplify EPIC. Break down your goal into manageable pieces and tackle them one at a time.

Be confident and brave and announce your plans to the world. Tell everyone what you are going to do. **Boldly proclaim your intentions and dreams!** You need to share your dreams so that you are accountable to people, but also so they can support you and celebrate with you when you succeed.

You should not walk your journey alone, but you absolutely must be your own best friend and biggest cheerleader. Do not waiver from believing in yourself and your ability to achieve your EPIC goals or dream. The positive voice in your head must drown out the naysayers. You must listen to and value the opinion of supportive people more than the wet blankets.

Adopt a growth mindset and *not yet* attitude. Not yet carries the promise of tomorrow. A growth mindset confirms gaining new skills and capacities are part of any truly EPIC journey.

You will achieve your goals more easily and faster if you **lean into your strengths** and leverage them. Use other people's strengths as well. Pour your time and energy into the things you love doing and are good at.

Outsource the things you do not enjoy doing and are not so good at. This will help keep you enthusiastic about your journey, but it also gives you the opportunity to invite accountability partners onto your team.

Have a plan that you revisit and revise often. Be adaptable. Expect setbacks and unexpected events and prepare for pivots and detours. Do not focus so much on a single route to your destination that you hit a brick wall with no place to go. Detours can present opportunities, and failures lessons. Roadblocks, detours, and failure are not reasons to quit. Keep a positive, ***not yet*** attitude. Do not give up on your dream. Simply remind yourself that you have not achieved it yet.

If you need cheerleaders, get stuck, or just want to interact with some like-minded EPIC seekers, then check out the *EPIC Begins* podcast, and log on to EPICbeginsnow.com. There is an entire community waiting to support you! If you found this book helpful, pass it on to a friend, and leave a book review online. That way, you will be helping others live an EPIC life, too.

You cannot control everything that happens to you or comes your way, but you are in control of how you respond. Life is full of choices; you are the champion of your own choices. Now choose to take the first step toward your EPIC goal or dream! **EPIC Choices, EPIC Life!**

*"Everything will be okay in the end. If
it is not okay, it is not the end."*

JOHN LENNON

ABOUT THE AUTHOR

ZANDER SPRAGUE is an award-winning public speaker, author, and Licensed Professional Clinical Counselor (LPCC). His mission is to help millions of people make the EPIC choices that create an EPIC life. Drawing on his decades of work experience with companies of all sizes, his education, and events in his own life, Zander guides people to achieve EPIC. With his talks, books, and courses, he helps people fulfill their potential and achieve their dreams.

Zander has a master's degree in Mental Health Counseling from Palo Alto University, and a Bachelor of Arts (BA) in History and Psychology from Pitzer College. He is a member of the National Speakers

Association, American Counseling Association, and California Association for Licensed Professional Clinical Counselors.

The author of three books, Zander is often a featured guest expert on podcasts and other broadcasts. His internationally acclaimed books include:

- *EPIC Begins With 1 Step Forward: Plan, Achieve, and Enjoy the Journey*
- *Making Lemonade: Choosing A Positive Pathway After Losing Your Sibling*
- *Why Don't They Cry?: Understanding Your Living Child's Grief*

His transformative training programs include:

- *EPIC Jumpstart*
- *30 Days to a Positive Pathway*™
- *EPIC Excellence*

Zander loves speaking to audiences around the world. Nicknamed the "God of Enthusiasm" because of his contagious energy and passion, he is a popular speaker, trainer, and podcast host. For more resources and content, visit www.ZanderSprague.com and www.EPICbegins.com. To book Zander to speak, email him at zander@zandersprague.com.